ACCIDENTS IN NORTH AMERICAN MOUNTAINEERING

VOLUME 7 • NUMBER 3 • ISSUE 51

1998

THE AMERICAN ALPINE CLUB
GOLDEN

THE ALPINE CLUB OF CANADA
BANFF

ISSN 0065-082X

ISBN 0-930410-79-3

Manufactured in the United States of America

Published by
The American Alpine Club, Inc.
710 Tenth Street, Suite 100
Golden, CO 80401

Cover Illustration
Featured on the front cover is a panorama of ice climbers—experienced and wanting to be—at what is now the Annual Ouray Ice Festival in Colorado. Many come here for their first outdoor climbing experience, having had their first exposure to the sport on indoor walls. Photographer: Lloyd Athearn, AAC Deputy Director.

♻ Printed on recycled paper

CONTENTS

SAFETY COMMITTEES 1997

The American Alpine Club

John Dill, Jeff Fongemie, Mike Gauthier, Jeff Sheetz, James Yester,
and John E. (Jed) Williamson *(Chairman)*

The Alpine Club of Canada

Tim Auger, David Dornian, Andre Kerkovius, Helmut Microys,
Mike Mortimer, and Murray Toft *(Chairman)*

ACCIDENTS IN
NORTH AMERICAN MOUNTAINEERING

Fifty-First Annual Report of the Safety Committees
of The American Alpine Club and The Alpine Club of Canada

Canada: Before moving to an overall view of the past year's Canadian accidents, there are two items of business I would like to mention. The first is the departure of Orvel Miskiw as Canadian editor. Orvel served as ANAM's Canadian correspondent for eight years, and the Alpine Club of Canada would like to thank him for the considerable effort he put into the position in that time. The second concerns the absence of the Canadian section in last year's publication due to production schedule difficulties. We are very happy to be back in this year's report, and apologize to any of last year's contributors who may have been concerned that their material was not included in the general publication. Statistics on last year's accidents are listed in the final sections of this year's report.

The frequency and severity of accidents reported in Canada over the past year have been consistent with a ten-year average, though there seem to be a few developments of note in terms of pattern of cause. Most striking is the increase in the number of people injured or killed in ice climbing accidents, but this is perhaps no surprise to anyone who climbs regularly in the Canadian Rockies (where most of these accidents have occurred). In the past few years there has been an obvious swell in the number of climbers on local waterfalls, and the increase in numbers may be the most direct and simple reason for the increase in accidents.

The second observation is that there has been a statistically significant increase in the number of climbers reported as "stranded." Whether this number reflects a decrease in the self-care capacities of climbers or an increase in climbers' ability to call in aid (through the carrying of cell phones, for example) is unclear, but the trend will be an interesting one to follow.

We thank the following people who contributed in various ways to this year's reporting: Tim Auger, Terry Barter, Will Devlin, George Field, Harry Fischer, Sylvia Forest, Gord Irwin, Martin Johansen, J.P. Kors, Marc Bedard, Marc Ledwidge, David Koonreeliusie, Sean Gesten, Darryl Paquette, Brad Sills, George Wallerstein, and Orvel Miskiw.

United States: This year seemed to be the year of many climbers being unable to self-arrest, either while on a "voluntary glissade" or after they slipped while climbing/descending. In most instances, a good belay would have been the best solution, as either the individuals were very new to glissading/climbing snow, or the conditions warranted it. Also in most cases, the runout was not very forgiving. These incidents accounted for over ten percent of the injuries.

The total number of accidents reported for the year is consistent with previous years, last year being an exception because only a few reports came forward for Washington. It has been pointed out before that not all the reports collected make it into the narratives.

There are a few reasons for this. First, the primary goal is to present descriptions and analyses that can be instructive to the readers. Second, there may be some human interest value—and even occasionally humor—that may suggest a lesson. Finally, the size of the report is designed to remain at a reasonable level. The hope is that such a policy will not discourage those who have a mishap from sending forward the particulars. While there are some contributors who indeed want to appear on these pages, there are others who clearly do not. Generally, I am impressed with the number of climbers who want to tell their stories so that others might not share the same fate. In this regard, the good news is that the report seems to be well received as an educational vehicle, even though there are no pictures or illustrations. A third printing of last year's edition suggests that interest in the subject matter is not waning.

There are many reports submitted that do not qualify as climbing accidents but may have interesting lessons to provide. A few of these are usually included. An example of one that was not included involved three 17-year-olds who decided to "go rappelling" on a 150-foot electrical tower. They were about ready to head home after one last rappel when the wind, at an estimated 30 mph, blew one of them into a coil. The 220,000 volt shock instantly burned off his shirt and harness, but he was able to sit on a cross beam over 100 feet off the deck for 45 minutes until rescued. He was successfully evacuated, but the second and third degree burns over 80 percent of his body resulted in his death two weeks later.

The concern here is that the inspiration for attempting this kind of feat may be generated from the media's recent fascination with climbing. Various venues—from desert towers to indoor walls—are being used for advertising, scenes for weekly television programs, and as whole segments for movies.

A couple of disturbing reports that one can only hope will not become a trend came from Seneca Rocks and Boulder Canyon. In the former, six climbers refused to help carry a litter down an easy part of the tourist trail, the technical part of the rescue having been completed. Their responses included: "I don't do that any more." "We're pretty tired." "I have to drive home." "We're in a hurry." In the latter location, a climber became angry when another climber was on "his" route and creating a hazard to his party. An altercation took place at the top. One climber was hospitalized with several lacerations caused by being struck with an ice ax. The attacker ended up in the Boulder County Jail.

In addition to the Safety Committee, we are grateful to the following individuals— with apologies for any omissions—for collecting data and helping with the report: Hank Alicandri, Aram Attarian, Micki Canfield, Hal Clifford, Greg Dillman, Ron Cloud, Jim Detterline, Renny Jackson, Tom McCrumm, Daryl Miller, Russell Peterson, Jim Schlinkmann, Steven Schmelzer, Jim Underwood, J. W. Wilder, and, of course, George Sainsbury.

John E. (Jed) Williamson
Managing Editor, USA
7 River Ridge Road
Hanover, NH 03755
e-mail: jedwmsn@sover.net

Geoff Powter
Editor, Canada
Box 8040
Canmore, Alberta T1W 2T8
email: gpowter@telusplanet.net

CANADA

FALL ON ICE, INADEQUATE PROTECTION, CLIMBING ALONE
Alberta, Waterton National Park, Expert's Choice

On February 10, a middle-aged male was attempting a solo ascent of the lower left pitch of Expert's Choice (WI4). He apparently was dragging a rope and performing a self-belay of some fashion when he fell about 20 meters, pulling out a number of screws on the way. Despite injuries to his hand, back and neck, he was able to walk or crawl down the trail to the roadway, where his wife was waiting. He was driven to hospital, where he remained for at least a month, with a broken finger and a broken vertebrae. (Source: Parks Canada Warden Service)

ROCKFALL
Alberta, Rocky Mountains, Cascade Waterfall

On Feb. 20, after a successful ascent of this waterfall (III, WI3), a party of three were setting up to rappel the route. A large rock (estimated at 50 to 80 lbs) came from above and hit one member in the head. He was wearing a helmet. He was knocked unconscious, and was bleeding from the ears. When he came to, his partners lowered him to the base of the route. A passerby on the highway noticed the evacuation and called the warden service. A rescue party was dispatched along with Banff EMS. The patient was stabilized on the trail and transported to the Banff hospital.

Analysis

The patient was later diagnosed with a depressed basal skull fracture. It is likely that wearing a helmet saved his life. (Source: Parks Canada Warden Service)

RAPPEL ERROR—INADEQUATE ANCHOR
Alberta, Bow Falls

On Feb. 23 around noon, a party of three were starting the descent of this Grade III, WI4 route. F.B. lowered J.P. and D.P. from a three-screw anchor. F.B. then proceeded to rappel from a single Simond 23-cm screw. The rope was draped over the head of the screw with the eye pointing up. A system was rigged on the screw which allows unwinding of the screw when the rope is retrieved. While on rappel, the anchor failed and F.B. fell about 60 feet onto shell ice on the intermediary ledge to which the first two had been lowered. He was complaining of a sore back. The rest of the party was assisted down by an ACMG guide also climbing the route. One person was sent to the trailhead to report the accident. A Warden Service rescue crew responded, and the injured climber was evacuated by heli-sling.

Analysis

Using a one-point rappel anchor can be risky. In this case the single screw and rope arrangement failed and it is likely that one of two things happened. Either the screw pulled out of the ice or the rappel rope slipped enough to wind the eye of the screw to a downward position, thus allowing the rope to slip off the head of the screw. If the latter happened, the rope would then continue to unwind the screw completely causing failure. The victim was fortunate that the shell ice he landed on absorbed some of his impact, likely minimizing his injuries. He was later diagnosed with only bruising injuries. (Source: Parks Canada Warden Service)

FALL ON ICE, DARKNESS, INADEQUATE TIE-IN AT ANCHOR
Alberta, Maligne Canyon
On March 18 at 2030, a party of three climbers were top- roping a waterfall in Maligne Canyon in Jasper National Park. One of the climbers was experienced, a second was intermediate, and the third was novice. The fact that they were climbing in the dark was intentional on their part, and they were using headlamps.

The last climber to finish the route was removing the anchors at the top of the climb when he fell approximately 25 meters to the canyon floor.

Park wardens were notified at 2100 by one of the climbers in the party. Wardens and paramedics were on the scene by 2130 and shortly thereafter the victim was pronounced dead. Rescue teams ground evacuated the victim from the canyon floor.

Analysis
It is difficult to determine the exact cause of the fall due to lack of direct observation, but wardens investigating the accident site believe the following scenario occurred:

Above the top of the waterfall, the ground slopes up steeply. A main anchor was established at the top of the waterfall. In order to set the top-rope anchor safely, the climbers had attached an 8mm line to a secondary anchor on the more level ground above the main anchor.

Two of the three climbers were at the bottom of the canyon, about to walk out. The third was at the top of the climb and was about to dismantle the system and hike out. He clipped into the safety line with a daisy chain attached to his harness, then dismantled the main anchor. At this point, he apparently leaned back against the safely line, thinking it still solid. With the main anchor removed however, the safety line was no longer attached at its bottom end. When the climber leaned back, he slid right down the safety line and off the end to the canyon floor.

Inexperience combined with climbing in the dark were key contributing factors in this accident. It is likely that with poor visibility the victim did not realize he had removed the integrity of the safety line when he dismantled the main anchor. (Source: Parks Canada Warden Service)

OVERDUE, FATIGUE, INADEQUATE EQUIPMENT, DARKNESS
Alberta, Murchison Falls
Three ice climbers set out to climb Murchison Falls (180m, V, WI4) at 1000, March 27, and were at the base of the first pitch at noon. One of the climbers was ill and returned to the highway, leaving the other two to complete the climb. They agreed to meet at the vehicle after the climb, but set no time, as they believed they would be down after dark.

At 1400 the pair were starting the third pitch. The ice was wet, and the climbers took three hours to climb the final 80 meters. Their only headlamp was left in a pack at the bottom of the climb, and they did not reach the top until dark. It took three hours for the pair to complete four rappels. By 2130 they were at the base of the climb, and were back at their vehicle by 2250. In the meantime, the third climber who had returned early became concerned, and at 2200 called the Jasper Park emergency line to request a rescue. Four wardens were on standby, and two responded to Saskatchewan Crossing where the reporting person was waiting. When wardens arrived, the climbers were safely down, and the rescue response was terminated.

Analysis
Although no rescue was required, this type of incident is becoming more common with the increase in popularity of ice climbing. Underestimating the time required to complete the climb, not retreating, having inadequate equipment, and fatigue all combined to result in a potentially serious incident. (Source: Parks Canada Warden Service)

FALL ON ROCK, INADEQUATE PROTECTION, EXCEEDING ABILITIES, OFF ROUTE
Alberta, Chinaman's Peak
On June 28, Allan J. (30) was leading pitch eight of the Northeast Face route (450m, 5.6) on Chinaman's Peak about 1300. He tried to go straight up from the belay instead of following the normal route, which would have seen him traverse up and right around a corner. The climbing became harder, but he continued until he slipped off, falling about 14 meters and ending up four meters below his belayer. He sustained a compound fracture of the left ankle.

Allan's two companions helped him up to the belay stance, and then one of them completed the climb and descended to get help. He flagged down Ranger MacLean on the road at 1430 to report the accident, and MacLean initiated a rescue. Shortly after 1515, three rangers and alpine specialists were slung to the accident site by helicopter. The victim was stabilized and evacuated to the Whiteman's Pass dam at 1610, then transported by Canmore EMS to the local hospital at about 1625. (Source: Kananaskis Country Alpine Specialist)

Analysis
It is unclear why the victim deviated from the normal route. This led directly to his inability to find protection and to the severity of his eventual fall. (Source: Geoff Powter)

FALL ON ROCK, NO HELMET, INADEQUATE PROTECTION, EXCEEDING ABILITIES, INEXPERIENCE
Alberta, Kananaskis Valley, Barrier Bluffs
Late in the afternoon of July 6, Justin W. (21) was top-roping The Wasp, a 5.9 route, on the Yellow Wall when he took a ten-meter fall. He was not wearing a helmet and suffered an open wound to the head. His sister, who was at the site, reported the accident to Ribbon Creek Emergency Center by cell phone, and a number of rangers reached the scene on foot in less than a half hour after the call. Justin was immobilized on a scoop stretcher, placed in a Baumann Bag, and moved out in the open to be accessible by helicopter sling. He was then flown down to the road, where he was transferred to an ambulance for transport to hospital.

Analysis
The reasons for the length of the victim's fall are unclear. Perhaps Justin had climbed past the top of the climb, or the rope had become unclipped at the top anchor. Justin

had learned to climb on indoor walls, and this was his first climb on real rock, so it's quite likely that his inexperience was a contributing factor. A helmet would likely have minimized or prevented the head wound. (Source: Kananaskis Country Alpine Specialist)

FALL ON ROCK—HAND HOLD CAME OFF, OFF ROUTE
Alberta, Castle Mountain, Goat Plateau Approach
On July 15, a party of two climbers scrambled up the standard approach for the Castle Mountain bivi hut. During the approach, they lost the rough trail and ended up off route in a series of cliff bands and gullies. The climbers were aware that they were off route but elected to continue, as they were on easy 5th Class terrain. The lower climber fell when a handhold broke away, and she tumbled several hundred meters down the mountain, suffering fatal head injuries. The Warden Service was contacted and evacuated the victim by helicopter.

Analysis
Neither climber was wearing a helmet at the time and the rope was stowed in the pack. While a helmet may not have prevented the massive head injury, the use of a rope may have. The victim was wearing a heavy pack at the time and this may have contributed to the fall. (Source: Parks Canada Warden Service)

FALL ON SNOW, INADEQUATE PROTECTION, FAULTY USE OF CRAMPONS
Alberta, Mount Andromeda
Two climbers had ascended Mount Andromeda and were descending via the Andromeda-Athabasca Col on July 31. Both climbers jumped across the bergschrund with crampons on. On the landing, one of the climbers caught her crampon and broke her ankle. The team was able to descend about 50 feet to more level ground. The uninjured climber descended the crevassed glacier and reported the incident. The climber was evacuated by helicopter and taken to EMS.

Analysis
This bergschrund poses many problems for climbers. Early in the season before the 'shrund opens up, many climbers try to jump across with crampons on, because it is less time consuming than setting up an anchor and rappelling. The consequence of jumping with crampons on is evident. (Source: Parks Canada Warden Service)

STRANDED, DIFFICULT TERRAIN, INSUFFICIENT RESEARCH
Alberta, Clemenceau to Chaba River Trek
An experienced party of eleven climbers flew in to the Clemenceau Icefield in August, spent five days climbing and exploring, and then started hiking out north toward the Banff-Jasper Highway. They made excellent progress over glaciated terrain, ending up on the West Chaba Glacier.

Their intent was to follow the West branch of the Chaba river to its confluence with the East Chaba River and thence down to the Athabasca River and out to the highway at Sunwapta Falls resort. However, the West Chaba river cuts a deep gorge below the glacier, and traveling beside or above this gorge is extremely treacherous.

The river was in flood, and crossing the river was out of the question. The group felt that to continue on their route would be unreasonably hazardous, and to backtrack would make any search efforts impossible. They therefore decided to stay put and wait for evacuation.

Due to the number of people in the party, the competent nature of the group, and the duration and complexity of the trip, it was felt by rescuers that being overdue by one day was not unreasonable. As a result, the party was given the better part of a day to hike out before a search was commenced. At 1700 on August 11, a search was started. With help from a detailed route plan provided to the searchers by the party prior to their departure, the rescue party was able to fly over the exact route the climbers intended to take, leading the searchers directly to the stranded group. The group was healthy and happy, but glad to see the helicopter, as they had been waiting at this campsite for three days and their food was getting low. The group was flown out to the highway.

Analysis
The group was experienced and the trip leader had done background research on the route. However the information he had received was from a winter perspective. The canyon which blocked their way would be hazardous but navigable in winter, but much more dangerous in summer.

Attempting to negotiate the gorge with this large group would have been unduly dangerous and difficult. Their decision to stop and wait for evacuation was the best they could have made in the circumstances. The group was so appreciative of the evacuation that they offered, and did pay for the helicopter evacuation. The money received from this group has gone directly into enhanced SAR training for public safety wardens. (Source: Parks Canada Warden Service)

FALL ON ROCK—ROCK DISLODGED, CLIMBING UNROPED
Alberta, Mount Neptuak
On August 10, a party of two were ascending the normal Northwest Ridge route on Mount Neptuak. The route is mostly loose 3rd and 4th Class, but is an exposed ridge on certain sections. While climbing a short, easy 5th Class step unroped, N.T. dislodged a hold, causing him to fall approximately 50 feet to lower angled terrain, then fell another 100 feet. He was killed in the fall. His partner returned to the hiking trail at Wenkchemna Pass and sent nearby hikers for help. A Warden Service rescue crew responded, and the deceased was evacuated by heli-sling.

Analysis
The route is technically easy, but is typical of the area because of loose rock and exposed sections. (Source: Parks Canada Warden Service)

STRANDED DUE TO SHOULDER DISLOCATION
Alberta, Mount Louis
On August 10, G.G. and G.B. were beginning the exit pitches on the summit tower of Mount Louis. They were attempting the classic Perren Variation (5.7). While starting to lead the first pitch, G.G. dislocated his shoulder and backed off the pitch. He was able to relocate the shoulder, but was unable to use the arm and continue.

The party called warden service dispatch on a cell phone and requested a rescue. A warden service rescue party responded by helicopter. The pilot was able to manage a partial landing on the ledge below the summit towers to evacuate the climbers. (Source: Parks Canada Warden Service)

(Editor's Note: More than a few climbers have the problem of chronic shoulder disloca-tion, though it is not certain whether that is the case here. The question is whether one can compensate for this problem by planning for it by having enough gear to rappel— which can be done with one arm incapacitated.)

FALL ON SNOW, CLIMBING UNROPED
Alberta, Mount Temple, Greenwood/Locke Route

On August 20, a party of two attempted the Greenwood/Locke Route (V, 5.9 A1). The two got a predawn start and reached the rock pitches above the upper icefield in good time. The pitches were very wet and they decided to retreat. They rappelled and down-climbed the majority of the lower route, then unroped to descend the final snow gully. The lowest climber was moving down the gully, facing out, when he lost his footing. He attempted to self-arrest and was partially successful. Before he could stop himself, a crampon hooked and he began to tumble, falling 200 meters to the scree below. His partner continued to descend the route and found his partner dead from massive head injuries. The second climber descended to the trail, and with the help of a cell phone from nearby hikers, contacted Warden Service Dispatch.

Analysis

Both climbers were very experienced. With the steepness of the descent gully and the short ice axes carried, it may have been better to descend the gully facing in, rather than out. (Source: Parks Canada Warden Service)

FALL ON ROCK, EXCEEDING ABILITIES, INADEQUATE PROTECTION, BELAY FAILURE
Alberta, Chinaman's Peak

On August 22, B.P. (20) and M.K. attempted to climb the usual Northeast Face of Chinaman's Peak when something went wrong, probably on the third or fourth pitch, and they both fell to their deaths.

The climbers were reported overdue by a friend of B.P. the next day, and a helicop-ter search of the area revealed their bodies at the base of the climb. Their equipment was spread throughout the area. The victims and most of their equipment were slung down to an ambulance at the parking area by the dam, and the operation was com-plete at 1300.

Analysis

Park Rangers deduced from the configuration of equipment that the leader had fallen and pulled the belayer from his station, but the reason for the leader's fall and the specif-ics of the anchor failure will unfortunately never be known. (Source: Kananaskis Coun-try Alpine Specialist)

LOST, CLIMBING ALONE, HYPOTHERMIA, WEATHER, INADEQUATE EQUIPMENT
Alberta, Columbia Icefield, Mount Athabasca

On Sept. 26, a lone climber took out a safety registration for a climb of Mount Athabasca, with a return time of 1200 the next day indicated, although the climber had no intention of over-nighting on the mountain. He was experienced, and successfully climbed the Silverhorn route. However, he was unfamiliar with the topography of the mountain, and a whiteout on the way up prevented him from viewing the standard descent route, which leaves the west ridge and follows a wide horizontal traverse to the right to avoid a large icefall.

From the summit, he started down the ridge toward the standard route, completely unaware of an alternative descent via the Athabasca-Andromeda Col, which could be reached by following the southwest branch of the same ridge down to the col. He had no trail to follow because of recent storm snow, and so traversed back and forth while descending, trying to find a way through the icefall. He did not go far enough down the ridge to find the traverse ramp, and was forced to bivouac at an elevation over 3000 meters, exposed to wind and snow overnight, with only a light nylon sack for protection.

When he failed to return on September 27, wardens became concerned, and proceeded at 1300 to search the mountain. By that time, the climber was severely hypothermic and unable to move, but he was able to wave his hand. The helicopter was prevented from landing by wind and poor visibility, so wardens were slung in under it to evacuate him. The pilot did a masterful flying performance in extremely poor conditions during the rescue. Paramedics who attended the victim estimate that he was within a half hour of death by hypothermia.

Analysis

Although the climber was experienced, he did not research the mountain adequately, and so became stymied when bad weather prevented him from seeing where to go. Had he known about the A-A Col descent route, or the correct line of the standard route, he might have gotten down on his own and in good time, even in bad weather. In any case, soloing on a glacier is hazardous. Many people have fallen into deep crevasses on Mount Athabasca. (Source: Parks Canada Warden Service)

RAPPEL ERROR—INCORRECT USE OF EQUIPMENT
Alberta, Smith-Dorrien Valley, Ranger Creek

At 1630 on November 9, authorities at Peter Lougheed Provincial Park received a radio call from M.P., who was at the scene of a rappelling accident on an ice climb on Mount Murray.

After a day of top-roping from a substantial anchor on an ice smear to the north of the R&D route in Ranger Creek, M.D. (36) had removed the carabiners from the top slings and threaded the climbing rope through two Abalakov loops before being lowered to the base by his belayer. During lowering, the climbing rope cut through the slings and M.D. fell to the bottom, sustaining extensive injuries: a broken femur, neck fractures, broken pelvis, a large puncture cut in the left knee, a compression fracture of the lower back and assorted cuts. He was in serious shock.

Park rangers drove to Ranger Creek, while a helicopter was dispatched from Canmore with an alpine specialist. Because of failing daylight and the severe injuries, a rescue had to be performed quickly. (Source: Kananaskis Country Alpine Specialist)

Analysis
Climbing ropes can easily cut through slings when they dynamically rub against each other. Most climbers are likely aware of the risk of this practice, yet some continue to take their chances with it. A rappel instead of a lower would have prevented this accident. (Source: Geoff Powter)

SLIP ON ICE, FAULTY USE OF CRAMPONS, CLIMBING UNROPED
Alberta, Smith-Dorrien Valley, French Creek
On November 20, L.S. (24) and a partner climbed an ice flow above French Creek on the east flank of Mount Burstall, about thirty minutes from the trailhead, and then proceeded to descend shortly before 1300.

While rappelling from the top to an icy ledge, one of L.S.'s crampons came off. Once on the ledge, the climbers decided to traverse and then scramble down rocks to the start of the climb. L.S. removed his other crampon and then started across the ledge, but slipped on the ice and tumbled about 15 meters down a low-angled part of the first pitch before free-falling another five meters to the base. He suffered a bad cut of the upper lip and teeth, complained of a sore right ankle, lower back, and neck, and could not remember falling, so he may have sustained a concussion as well, although his helmet stayed on.

L.S. tried to leave the area, but his pain was too great, even with help, so his companion went out to the road and flagged down Ranger Scott in the Chester Lake parking lot to ask for help in evacuating Lee. Authorities requested a helicopter, and the victim was fitted with a C- collar, then lifted by sling in a scoop stretcher and Baumann Bag to a road ambulance at 1630. He was treated by paramedics, then taken to Canmore Hospital. (Source: Kananaskis Country Alpine Specialist)

Analysis
It may have served the victim better to keep his remaining crampon on; the ice on the ledge proved to be far more slippery than anticipated. (Source: Geoff Powter)

FALL ON ICE, INADEQUATE PROTECTION, SELF-BELAY FAILURE
Alberta, Kananaskis Valley, Kidd Falls
On November 23, S.M. (21) and a partner set off to climb the big waterfall below Mount Kidd's Gunbarrel Gully above Galatea Creek, obvious from Kananaskis Highway 40 south of the mountain. Early in the day, S.M. was leading high above his belay, when he stopped to place a screw for protection. While doing so, his tools pulled and he fell some 20 meters, sustaining two fractured and one crushed vertebrae. He was unconscious for approximately five minutes, but then revived, complaining of back pain. He had a deformity in the thoracic region of his back, so his partner left him at the base of the falls to hike out for help, and called Kananaskis Emergency Services about noon. (Source: Kananaskis Country Alpine Specialist)

Analysis
The condition of the ice on this warm day may have contributed to the victim's tools pulling. Placing protection lower on the climb would have perhaps prevented the victim from hitting the bottom of the climb. (Source: Geoff Powter)

FALL ON ICE, INADEQUATE PROTECTION
Alberta, Mount Rundle, The Professor Falls
On November 23, R.R. was leading the second pitch of this popular Grade III, WI4 route. About twenty feet up the second pitch, he placed his second screw but did not like the placement. He then placed a third screw to back it up, clipped it and then put his weight on it. Both screws failed and he fell to the bottom of the pitch injuring his knee. His partner and nearby climbers lowered him to the base of the route. His partner then went for help. He was evacuated with heli-sling by park warden rescue crew shortly after. (Source: Parks Canada Warden Service)

Analysis
The dependability of protection in ice is sometimes circumspect, occasionally to the point that apparently good screws will hold little better than body weight in poor ice. The possibility of gear failure needs to be factored into decisions about frequency and location of screw placements. (Source: Geoff Powter)

RAPPEL ERROR—INADEQUATE PROTECTION
Alberta, Rocky Mountains, Mount Murchison, Murchison Falls
On November 23, a party of two were beginning the rappel descent of this waterfall route (180m, V, WI4). On their third rappel, the first climber got part way down the ropes, yelled, and fell down a few hundred feet to the bottom of the route. His partner (along with another nearby party of two) continued down uneventfully. They determined from his massive head injuries that P.E. was dead and walked out for assistance. They reported the accident late that night to the Warden Service. The victim was evacuated the next morning by heli-sling.

Analysis
The climber was not using a prussik to back up his rappel and he was using an ATC to rappel on two 8.5mm ropes. The ends of the rappel ropes were not knotted. When rappelling on small diameter ropes, extra caution must be used as there is less friction and it is therefore easier to lose control of the rappel. In this case it is possible that the ropes were wet or iced, and that may have contributed to losing control of the rappel. Having no backup did not leave any room for error. (Source: Parks Canada Warden Service)

FALL ON SNOW, CLIMBING UNROPED, FAILURE TO FOLLOW INSTRUCTIONS
British Columbia, Mount Revelstoke National Park, Mount Macbeth
On June 29, a relatively experienced climber, upon reaching the summit of Mount Macbeth, unroped and fell through the cornice. His body was recovered by heli-sling the following day approximately 330 meters below.

Analysis
Other members of the party stayed roped at the same location, and stated that they advised the victim to also remain tied in. He did not listen to their advice, and then stepped into an area that the others said they would not go near because of obvious cornice potential.

Why the victim chose to forsake both the advice and risk the obvious hazard is unknown, though he had apparently demonstrated some risky behaviour on previous outings as well. (Source: Parks Canada Warden Service; Nelson B.C. RCMP Detachment personnel)

AVALANCHE, FALL INTO CREVASSE, POOR POSITION, WEATHER, INADEQUATE PREPARATION
British Columbia, Mount Robson

A party of three (Party One) and a party of two (Party Two) were climbing Mount Robson via the Kain route on July 9. They set up camp in whiteout conditions, knowingly in an icefall area, but uncertain as to their exact location. The campsite was in a heavily crevassed area below seracs. Three climbers over-nighted in a tent while two members of Party One bivied nearby.

At 0610, a falling serac caused a class 3.5 avalanche, which swept the tent and occupants down the slope approximately 100 meters. One of the climbers bivouacking was swept down 40 meters, and the second bivouacker was swept into a crevasse just below the bivi site. He landed on a snow bridge 12 meters down in the crevasse. The remainder of the party conducted a search for the missing climber for 1.5 hours without success, then walked to Berg Lake Ranger Station to report the incident.

Park wardens responded from Jasper to Mount Robson, while Robson park rangers conducted a reconnaissance flight over the area. First party responders landed at the bottom of the avalanche path and began to search the debris; the second party, consisting of wardens and two avalanche search dogs, flew to the top of the path and searched in the vicinity of the campsite. The missing climber was located near the campsite in a crevasse, and a warden was lowered in to recover the body.

Analysis

The party set up camp in white-out conditions and were not aware of their exact location. The camp was established in an area of very high objective hazard. Icefall caused a class 3.5 avalanche which swept over the campsite area. The experience level of the combined groups was intermediate, with poor map reading skills. They did not have transceivers. Consultations before departure with readily available local resources about the placement of camps and their relative dangers would have been helpful. (Source: Parks Canada Warden Service)

FALL INTO RIVER
British Columbia, Jasper National Park, North Boundary Trail Hike

D.H. and S.K. (from Germany) were hiking the north boundary trail of Jasper National Park. The summer had been extremely rainy and the rivers were all in flood. On July 12, they had crossed over Snake Indian Pass and were heading down valley to a campsite on the shores of Twintree Creek. The campsite was flooded due to high water levels in the creek. Normally this creek can be crossed with high gumboots, but at this time, the water was very high and fast. A foot bridge, consisting of two stringers, was in place to cross the creek, but water was overlapping the bridge. Deciding to push on to the next campsite, S.K. started to cross the bridge by straddling it, and shuffling across it. Once across, D.H. started across using the same technique. Both women were carrying heavy packs with waist straps done up.

Midway across, D.H. got stuck on a knot on one of the logs, and could not proceed.

With cold water lapping up to her waist, she soon lost strength and let go, falling into the creek. She floated down a short way, and was able to grab onto a sweeper, but again lost her grip, and was carried down stream. Meanwhile, S.K. attempted to help her, but eventually lost sight of her. She combed the shore for two hours, then proceeded to hike out for help. It took her two days to reach Mount Robson Park ranger station, (very good time) where she reported the incident. Park wardens from Jasper were notified at 1700 on July 14, and flew in to search the area for D.H. They were unable to find the body that night, but the following day, the body was located in a log jam about 70 meters downstream of the footbridge.

Analysis
Although not a climbing incident per se, this episode is included here because climbers often have to approach their objectives by crossing streams, and can treat these crossings as minor, rather than serious, obstacles. Although this creek in this incident is usually very benign, flooding from a month of heavy rain caused it to become a wild torrent. Even though it was late in the afternoon, D.H. and S.K. felt obliged to push on to the next campsite, as the upper campsite was flooded. Had they either made do in the wet campsite and tried crossing the bridge in the morning when the water level was lower, or at least undone the waist bands on their packs, this incident may have been avoided. (Source: Parks Canada Warden Service)

FALL INTO MOAT, FALLING ROCK, WEATHER
British Columbia, Bugaboo Glacier Provincial Park, Bugaboo Spire
In August, S.A. and B.C. approached the east face of Bugaboo Spire, intending to climb the Left-Hand Herr route. They ascended a snow apron below the face, crossed a bergschrund, and reached a moat, which was the final obstacle before the actual rock climbing. They proceeded to cross the moat to a small ledge on the rock. B.C. stepped across and was moving up to the ledge when S.A. attempted to cross the moat. She stepped on a small snow bridge that was supporting a boulder, and the bridge collapsed, releasing the boulder. It slowly rolled onto her and pushed her some three meters down into the moat. S.A. managed to wriggle out from under the boulder and climb to the surface, but soon collapsed from massive internal injuries, and eventually required CPR. Other climbers in the area quickly responded to assist. The accident was reported to the Park Rangers, and S.A. was transported to Invermere Hospital via helicopter, but was pronounced dead upon arrival.

Analysis
This accident may have been avoided if the snow bridge had not been used; the day was extremely warm and all snow bridges should have been suspect. Warm weather throughout the previous week likely made snow support of all boulders suspect as well. (Source: Bugaboo Glacier Provincial Park Ranger)

FALLING ROCK, WEATHER
British Columbia, Bugaboo Glacier Provincial Park, Bugaboo—Snowpatch Col
A party of three, N.G., J.G., and G.W., was ascending to the Bugaboo-Snowpatch Col using a rope at 0800 on August 4. A boulder slid down the slope above them with almost no warning, glanced off G.W. and struck N.J. squarely.

J.G. self-arrested the party and immediately provided first aid. N.G. had sustained a broken left femur and fractured right arm, and G.W. a hand injury. Another nearby climber ran to the B.C. Parks Kain Hut and alerted park rangers. Assistance was requested from the Parks Canada Warden Service. A warden service rescue team responded from Banff, and the patient was heli-slung from site and then flown to Brisco to a waiting ambulance. The climber who ran for help fell while running and injured his ribs. He was flown to the trailhead and met by his partner.

Analysis
This is the usual route to access the west side of the spires. Rockfall (natural and climber-generated) is common there and is potentially a major hazard. Extremely warm temperatures in the days preceding the incident likely contributed to the spontaneous release of this large rock. (Source: Parks Canada Warden Service; Bugaboo Glacier Provincial Park Ranger; George Wallerstein, Participant).

FALLING ROCK—PULLING RAPPEL ROPE DOWN, POOR POSITION
British Columbia, Bugaboo Glacier Provincial Park, Snowpatch Spire
In August, a party of three climbers had completed the final rappel after climbing the Kraus-McCarthy route on Snowpatch Spire, and were standing at the base while the rope was pulled down. The rope dislodged a rock the size of a grapefruit, and A.B. was struck on the forearm. His companions conducted first aid and assisted A.B. to the Kain Hut. The injury was not serious, and he regained movement of the arm and hand in a few days.

Analysis
The potential existed for this situation to have been much more serious, as a rock of that size falling from any more than a few meters can be a deadly missile, and a helmet may not be effective against it. Pulling of a rope always requires constant vigilance for rockfall. (Source: Bugaboo Glacier Provincial Park Ranger)

LIGHTNING
British Columbia, Bugaboo Glacier Provincial Park, Snowpatch Spire
A.B. and B.A. were descending the Kraus-McCarthy rappel route in August when an electrical storm developed. Lightning struck the top of the Spire when they were about four rope lengths down the route. A.B. was rappelling, and part of the charge migrated down the wet crack system of the route. A.B. received a shock and lost consciousness, but his rappel back-up device held him. After he regained consciousness a short time later, the two continued rappelling the route. Luckily, no serious injuries occurred as a result of the ground current.

Analysis
Lightning storms are a constant threat in the Bugaboos and can quickly form without warning. The crack system of the Kraus-McCarthy route notoriously acts as a terrain lightning funnel, with the crack in the corner of the route wet even on dry days. Fortunately this party was well down below the peak when it was struck, and were rappelling from an exposed position to a safer position off the spire itself. They were thus exposed

to only a small fraction of the current delivered by the strike. This incident is a strong reminder to back up a rappel with a self-arresting device. (Source: Bugaboo Glacier Provincial Park Ranger)

FALL ON ROCK, ROPE PARTED—FRICTION DEVICE
Northwest Territories, Baffin Island, Mount Thor

In mid-July A.G. (30) began a solo attempt on a new route on the 3800-foot granite west face. The lower two thirds of the face are vertical and the upper third is overhanging with an average angle of 105 degrees. Another party of two climbers was also climbing a new route on the face which they completed in late August. When they returned to the valley on August 23, they called in to Auyittuk Park headquarters on a radio in an emergency shelter to report that they had not seen or heard from the solo climber since early August. A Canadian Armed Forces Labrador rescue helicopter was in the area and was dispatched to do a reconnaissance of the face. Remnants of a camp were spotted on the end of the prominent ledge dividing the vertical and overhanging sections of the face. There was no sign of the missing climber. It was decided that the face could not be accessed by helicopter due to its steepness.

Since there is no local technical mountain rescue capability, the Parks Canada Warden Service Mountain Rescue Unit in the Canadian Rocky Mountain National Parks was contacted for assistance. A rescue team along with a certified rescue pilot was dispatched and flew by commercial air from Calgary, Alberta to Pangnirtung, Northwest Territories. Arrangements were made to have a locally chartered Bell Long Ranger 3 available for the crew.

After an initial reconnaissance of the face and the remnants of the camp were spotted, it was decided that inserting two rescuers onto the ledge on the face was possible. The ledge was wide enough at one point that, using a 50-foot line, there would be enough clearance for the helicopter. Once on the ledge the two rescuers scrambled over to the old bivi site where the missing climber was found lying dead in a pile of boulders. He had fallen about 50 feet. His rope was broken above the self- belay device he had been using (a Rock Exotica Solo-Aid).

It was not possible to sling into the victim's location due to the overhanging wall. For this reason, a rope was tied to the body and laid out along the ledge to the point where it could be picked up safely by the 50-foot sling rope underneath the helicopter. The body was evacuated to the staging area, and the two rescuers were then slung off the face.

Analysis

After completing the investigation and after talking to a number of people about solo aid climbing, the rescue team speculated that the following is what likely occurred.

The accident happened on August 3. The fatal fall was a result of the victim's rope parting. The break in the rope near the self belay device clearly showed this. The other end of the rope could be seen fifty feet higher, with about two feet dangling from the last aid piece. Due to the overhanging nature of the wall and the logistics of solo aid leading, the rope was being clove-hitched to the gear placements as the climber moved up. Because of these direct tie-offs, the fatal fall created a Factor Two force on a short section of rope.

It is unlikely, however, that the rope was broken by the self-belay device. We conclude this because the broken segment of rope above the self-belay device was bunched up and rigid and the broken end was about 12 inches away from the jaws of the belay device. If the self-belay device had broken the rope, the rigid rope should have been behind the device.

It is therefore speculated that the climber was also using an ascender above his belay device. The broken end near the self-belay device showed signs of heat damage consistent with cutting by an ascender. Unlike a self-belay device, an ascender is not designed or intended to absorb a fall—particularly a Factor Two fall. The propensity for ascenders to cut ropes combined with the rope damage which his ropes would have sustained from the first 2000 feet of difficult aid climbing are likely the reasons why the rope broke. The wear to the ropes is substantiated by a diary entry. (Source: Parks Canada Warden Service)

FALL INTO MOAT, CLIMBING UNROPED, POOR POSITION, INEXPERIENCE
Québec, Saint Raymond de Portneuf, Delaney Falls

On January 13, E.F. and E.L. had just finished climbing La Transparente, a 150m waterfall climb on Delaney Falls near St. Raymond de Portneuf. They had both reached the top of the falls by about 1210, and where an easy slope continued upward for another few meters, E.F. unroped and began to walk toward the top.

E.L. collected their equipment before continuing up to meet his partner for lunch. He suddenly noticed he could no longer see or hear his partner and began searching for him. He eventually found a hole in the ice of the slope that he suspected his partner may have fallen into. He could see nothing, but calling into the water rushing into the hole, realized he could communicate with E.F.

E.L. dropped a rope into the hole, and E.F. confirmed he was able to tie into the rope. E.L. was unable, however, to rig an extraction system, and so had to find another way to get to his partner. He descended about five meters and made a hole through the ice, but was still unable to see E.F.

E.L. returned to the top of the climb to attempt to pull the rope from a different direction, again without luck. He returned to the hole he had previously made in the ice, and could now see the rope in it, indicating that E.F. had slipped farther down behind the ice. E.L. realized that some time had passed, that he was unlikely to be able to extricate his partner himself, and that he still had a long snowshoe and drive to get to rescue authorities. He tied his partner off and went off to call the police.

The Québec Police Intervention Group was called to initiate a rescue. At the scene of the accident, the rescuers attempted to raise the victim with the help of a winch connected to the rope which he had previously tied to his seat harness. The technique worked until E.F.'s body apparently jammed.

The police then set up a rope some 15 meters below, where there was a natural hole through the ice. They hoped to try again from there with the help of a sledge hammer and an ax, but as it was late in the day by then and darkness would increase the hazard to rescuers, they postponed further efforts until morning.

It took two days before the police located and recovered the body. At Portneuf Central Hospital, Dr. Céline Cantin could do no more than pronounce E.F. dead at 1400. (Source: Jacques Kirouac (FQME); Marc Bedard, Québec Coroner)

Analysis

This incident attracted a considerable amount of attention in the popular press in Québec, bringing out calls for regulation, mandatory certification of climbers and even the banning of climbing in the area. The strength of these suggested remedies is somewhat out of proportion to the simple steps that might have been taken to avoid the incident in the first place.

Usually, when a significant amount of water is flowing inside or behind a waterfall, it can be seen or heard, and flowing water should warn climbers of thin ice. The victim did not consider the hazard of walking on the ice adequately, and left himself unprotected when he unroped and trusted the crust.

The first step in a crevasse-type accident like this should have been to secure the victim's rope to protect him from falling farther. If E.L. had known some simple crevasse-rescue techniques, he may have been able to extricate his friend or help him climb out and save him. Many climbers in non-glaciated areas never learn these techniques, which is unfortunate, because crevasse rescue practices can be easily adapted for safety in non-glacial situations. (Source: Geoff Powter)

FALL ON ROCK, INADEQUATE PROTECTION
Québec, Mount Saint Hilaire, Dame Noire Route

On May 31, M.L. (33), with six years of climbing experience, and C.M. were attempting Dame Noire (5.8). M.L. was leading in a dihedral, six meters above his second and last placement, and placing protection in a crack system, when his right foot suddenly slipped on some wet moss. His left hand also slipped and he fell off. He had just enough time to push himself away from the rock, but still hit his right and then his left foot against the rock as he dropped.

According to his belayer, M.L. was face-down before being stopped by the rope two meters below the belay station, a total fall of about twelve meters. M.L. tied himself in to the belay system with a sling, rested a few minutes, and then belayed his partner while he retrieved their equipment. M.L. then rappelled to the ground, where C.M. administered first aid and assessed his injuries. He had sustained a fracture of the right foot and a traumatic bursitis of the left ankle. (Source: Jacques Kirouac, FQME)

Analysis

This climb was reportedly well within M.L.'s ability, so he may have pushed his lead out as a result. A six-meter runout is excessive so close to the ground. Fortunately, his top piece held, as C.M. reported that the other chock had nearly fallen out of the crack, as it was held in only by the cable. The injuries may have been lessened or nullified if the leader had placed more protection. (Source: Orvel Miskiw)

UNITED STATES

RAPPEL ERROR—ROPE TANGLED, STRANDED, INEXPERIENCE, DARKNESS, INADEQUATE EQUIPMENT—NO HEAD LAMP
Alabama, Pelham

On March 2, Chad Lovelady (23) and Eric Langwager (17) decided they would go rappelling that evening on rocks behind the building where they work. Around 9:00 pm, Chad began the first rappel. About mid-way down, he noticed an overhand knot in the line. Rather than remove it, he forced it through his figure eight, continued to the bottom, and then asked Eric to remove it before descending. Eric untied the knot, tossed the rope down and began his rappel, with Chad on belay. Since it was dark and they were using a black rope, neither one could see that the rope had tangled about 60 feet from the bottom. Eric stopped just above the entanglement and tried to remove it with one hand. Due to his inexperience, he did not know how to lock off, so he tired and quickly slipped closer to the jam. This forced Chad to tighten the belay, which cinched the entanglement even more.

Rescue was called around 8:30 pm by a third party. After a basic pick-off, the climbers went on their way.

Analysis

Chad had about six years of experience, but Eric had only one month. Chad felt the entanglement was attributable to the fact the rope had been twisted by his figure-eight ring on the first rappel, and to the lack of attention when the rope was tossed off. The inability to correct the problem was also the result of rappelling at night without headlamps. (Source: Matthew Mobley, Pelham Fire Department)

HACE, INADEQUATE COMMUNICATION—CLIENT TO GUIDE
Alaska, Mount McKinley, West Buttress

An Alaska Denali Guiding Party led by Blaine Smith took ten days to reach the 14,200 foot camp on the West Buttress of Mount McKinley, arriving May 23. Jack Miller (45), a client in the party, experienced Acute Mountain Sickness his third night at 11,000 feet and his first night at 14,200 feet on May 23. He did not communicate the extent of his problem with the guides. Another client in the party developed Pulmonary Edema which was diagnosed at the 14,200 foot Ranger Camp on May 24. Miller spent an equally miserable night over the 24th. By the morning of the 25th, Miller told Smith of his condition. Miller was very hypoxic when he was taken to the 14,200 foot Ranger Station and examined by volunteer physician Ken Zafren at 1230. Miller said that he had blood in his urine two previous days after making carries. Zafren recommended that Miller not go any higher soon and spend the day taking it easy, possibly walking around camp. The party spent the day in practice just a short distance from camp. For the remainder of the day, Miller walked around camp, but became increasingly ill from AMS. Several times he collapsed, experiencing extreme headache, nausea, and vomiting. Smith returned from practice about 1830. Miller stated, "I'm feeling better, I've been walking around

4

today." One hour later, Miller said, "I don't feel so good," so Smith took Miller back to see Dr. Zafren at 2000. Miller was mildly ataxic and was told that he may have to go down. Miller returned to his camp and in one hour he became extremely ataxic. Miller was assisted back to see Dr. Zafren where he collapsed outside of the medical tent at 2115. Miller was diagnosed with extreme High Altitude Cerebral Edema requiring an immediate evacuation to a lower elevation. Ranger Roger Robinson requested the contract LAMA helicopter for the evacuation from Talkeetna. Miller's condition continued to deteriorate over the next hour. Miller was flown straight to Talkeetna where he was transported by ambulance to Valley Hospital in Palmer. Miller's condition improved dramatically upon descent to sea level, but it took him ten days to get back his coordination and most of his memory of the incident.

Analysis
Jack Miller had never ascended above 7,000 feet prior to his climb so his ability to acclimatize was an unknown. Most people will acclimatize to 14,000 feet if given ten days to reach this height. Miller should have confided with Blaine Smith his difficulty with acclimatizing. This life threatening evacuation could have been avoided since he could have descended with the other clients and guide on the 24th. (Source: Roger Robinson, Mountaineering Ranger)

AMS—NO INCIDENT
Alaska, Mount McKinley, West Buttress
Kim Jae Suk and Park Jae Il (24) of the Korean Palgong Kyung Ju party ascended the Messner Couloir on May 28. Il became ill with Acute Mountain Sickness over half way up the route, requiring eighteen hours to reach the top at midnight. At 0105 on the 29th, Suk requested a helicopter evacuation for Il from the 19,400 foot level. Two other members in the Palgong party ascended from 17,200 feet on the West Buttress to provide assistance. Once they reached Il, they were able to determine that he could descend with their assistance. At 0340, they radioed out this information and that no rescue was needed. Il descended safely with their support.

Analysis
Here's a good example of team effort and self-sufficiency. With a little prompting, the rescue pair was more than willing to climb up through the cold hours of the evening to help a team member. In so many other rescues, climbers either give up or assume they will be rescued. It was a relief to see this Korean party work together to assist their ill person down. (Source: Roger Robinson, Mountaineering Ranger)

OFF ROUTE, FALL ON SNOW—UNABLE TO SELF-ARREST, NO BELAY/ PROTECTION
Alaska, Mount McKinley, West Buttress
At 0800 on May 29, the "British Army Expedition" departed the 17,200 foot camp with three members: Dr. Martin Kitson, Paul Holmes, and expedition leader Mark Trevillyan (20s). Expedition member Matthew Yorke stayed in camp deciding not to attempt the summit. The "BAME" expedition had departed the 7,200 foot Kahiltna base camp on May 15 and had spent four days acclimating at 14,000 feet before climbing up to the high camp at 17,200 feet.

At 1400, Kitson decided to turn back and head to the 17,200 foot camp. Kitson was experiencing headaches and felt that his condition would worsen if he continued to climb higher. Trevillyan and Holmes continued on to the "football field" at 19,600 feet. Holmes said that at 1630 the weather closed in and the visibility became poor. They were descending from the "football field" when they got off route due to the poor visibility. Holmes realized that after sliding on the steep snow for about 50 feet and stopping that they were on the wrong route. Holmes said that at 1800 he and Trevillyan got together to discuss their predicament. They both decided at that time they needed to traverse off the snow slope they were on and attempt to get back on the West Buttress. The weather at the time was extreme, with ambient temperatures at -10 F and winds gusting at 30 MPH. After talking several minutes, they started descending and traversing when a snow slab under their feet gave way and both Holmes and Trevillyan began falling and then tumbling, smashing through several rock bands.

Holmes recalls waking up at 2130 with Trevillyan lying on top of him with their climbing rope and other gear tangled and wrapped around them. Holmes checked Trevillyan for a pulse and other vital signs. Holmes, a licensed British Army Medic, stated that Trevillyan failed to respond, was blue in skin color, had no signs of life after shaking him for several minutes and yelling his name, and had no pulse. After several minutes Holmes placed his pack below Trevillyan for a marker in case his body could be recovered. Holmes began shouting and attempted to crawl for help. Holmes said he was totally disoriented and unsure of his whereabouts.

At 2200, Climber Chris Eng of the "Eng Expedition" was looking for his partner when he heard Holmes shouting and started climbing toward him. Eng, who was totally disoriented also because of whiteout conditions, had been searching since 0800. He had followed a wanded trail to the bottom of the Messner Couloir and found two ski poles with large baskets. He assumed he was at the bottom of the fixed lines at 15,200 feet. Eng climbed toward the shouting and said that Holmes could barely walk when he first observed him. Climber Penn Burris found Eng and Holmes and started to lead them both back to the 14,200 foot Ranger Camp.

At 0100 on May 30, Burris, Eng and Holmes arrived at the 14,200 foot Ranger Camp. Holmes was examined by Dr. Ken Zafren and was kept at the medical tent overnight.

At 0930 on May 31, Holmes was flown by the NPS LAMA helicopter to the 7,200 foot Kahiltna base camp. He was then transported by a Pavehawk Air National Guard helicopter to an Anchorage hospital where he was admitted for several days. Trevillyan's body was recovered and flown off the mountain.

Analysis
Trevillyan and Holmes paid a heavy price for descending the Orient Express by mistake. They also committed another error that has injured many and has taken the lives of 29 climbers to date on Mount McKinley: they were roped together, descending on steep terrain, and had no fixed or running protection to stop their fall in case they could not self-arrest. (Source: Daryl Miller, Mountaineering Ranger)

FROSTBITE, WEATHER
Alaska, Mount McKinley, West Buttress
On May 31, a guided group of five clients led by Blaine Smith and Willy Peabody of Alaska Denali Guiding, was forced to spend the night out in a storm at 19,000 feet on

Mount McKinley. Due to this emergency bivouac four of the clients suffered second, third, and fourth degree frostbite on hands, feet and noses and required a National Park Service helicopter rescue. Several of the clients suffered tissue loss resulting from their frostbite.

Analysis

Rapidly deteriorating weather conditions at the higher elevations on Mount McKinley have historically been contributing factors to serious accidents. This particular event led to the first fatality of the season. According to Ranger Roger Robinson who was stationed at the 14,200 foot camp, "The storm moved in very fast to 14,200 feet, movement in and out of the camp was nearly impossible due to strong winds and zero visibility."

The decision to make a summit attempt on that morning was based on years of mountain experience and twelve previous summit trips that Blaine Smith had led. Ten groups successfully reached the summit on May 29, and one decided to turn around at the "football field." Adrian Clarke was descending from his first summit of Mount McKinley when he passed the ADG group on Pig Hill. Clarke reported that he was surprised to see a guided tour still ascending in the marginal weather. The most ominous precursor to the severe weather was the wind shift from a northerly to a southerly. This change did not occur until the party was on the summit ridge. It is not always possible to wait for a bluebird day to make a summit attempt; hence, decisions must be made by evaluating the conditions and the group at hand.

One action that may have enabled the group to descend to Denali Pass more quickly would have been to place more wands at closer intervals on their ascent. If Smith had forced on into such conditions or they had not had the tools to shelter themselves, this incident would have been more serious. To the credit of the guides, there were no fatalities. (Source: Joe Reichardt, Mountaineering Ranger)

FROSTBITE, WEATHER
Alaska, Mount McKinley, Muldrow Glacier

On June 4, at 1130, Wendt Andreas (34) of the High Dreams expedition checked in at the 14,000 foot Ranger Camp. Andreas had frozen all his fingers on both hands. His companions Mario Bornschein and Holger Kloss also sustained first degree frostbite to their fingers, but did not need to be evacuated.

The High Dream expedition planned a traverse of the mountain, starting from the Muldrow Glacier and descending the West Buttress. On the way up the Muldrow Glacier route, the group was moving up in good weather when a quick forming storm caught them on an exposed section of the route. They were forced to put up their tent for protection from the wind. The tent pole broke during the storm, and the group was forced to move until they could dig a snow shelter.

It is believed that all three sustained their frostbite injuries during their forced movement from the tent site, and while digging their snow shelter.

The three climbers went up and over Denali Pass and down the West Buttress route to the 14,000 foot Ranger Camp. At the Ranger Camp, patrollers evaluated and treated Andreas. A helicopter evacuation was requested to avoid further trauma to Andreas' hands. Andreas was flown to base camp (7,000 feet) where Doug Geeting Aviation flew him to Talkeetna.

Analysis

Storms on Denali often occur without obvious warning. The High Dreams expedition experienced one such phenomenon. (Source: Kevin Moore, Mountaineering Ranger)

AVALANCHE, WARM WEATHER
Alaska, Mount Hunter, Moonflower Buttress

On June 6, at 1700, Allan Kearney and Steve Mascioli (38) were climbing during a warm weather spell on the North Buttress Moonflower route of Mount Hunter. Allan was leading the 17th pitch of this technically demanding climb with Steve Mascioli belaying when a massive snow block broke loose above Mascioli, striking him. Kearney was able to instantly see that Mascioli's body had sustained major trauma and blood loss, and that he was dead. Kearney was pulled backward to his last piece of protection by the force of the falling snow block. He then worked his way down and retrieved the haul bag along with other climbing gear. Kearney was unable to cut Mascioli loose because he was too far below him after descending to retrieve the haul bag. Kearney then rappelled to his bivy site on the 15th pitch. He assembled additional gear necessary to descend, and then began rappelling the route.

He rappelled to the fifth pitch, reaching it on June 8. He then stayed at the fifth pitch, while avoiding further snow avalanches caused by the warm conditions. Kearney stayed there for approximately half a day, then noticed that below him there was a tent site with other climbers and that the other climbers were preparing to leave. Kearney began yelling down to the other party to wait for him so he could rope up with them for the descent of the Southeast Fork of the Kahiltna Glacier. One of the climbers Kearney yelled down to was Eli Helmuth. Helmuth radioed Eric Martin at the 7,200 foot base camp using a CB radio. Helmuth told Martin that it appeared a single climber rappelling above him was in need of some type of assistance. Martin contacted the Talkeetna ranger station and advised them of the situation, and that poor weather prevented any type of aerial rescue.

Ranger Daryl Miller advised Ranger Martin to make preparations for a possible ground rescue. Preparations for a possible ground rescue were made at base camp while Helmuth attempted to get further information from the party above him. Helmuth again contacted base camp and notified Martin that no further assistance was needed, as Kearney's partner was dead and Kearney was uninjured. Kearney, Helmuth and Helmuth's climbing partner returned to base camp, arriving at 2120.

On June 11, NPS staff JD Swed, Joe Reichert and Dave Kreuzer did a series of reconnaissance flights over the site using the NPS LAMA helicopter. They determined that a recovery attempt would be feasible. NPS ranger Joe Reichert, using short-haul technique, successfully recovered Mascioli's body. Mascioli's body was transported from the 7,200 foot base camp to Talkeetna by Hudson Air Service, and then transported along with three gear bags belonging to Mascioli to Kehl's Palmer Mortuary.

Analysis

The North Buttress Moonflower route on Mount Hunter is one of the most technically difficult and demanding climbing routes in the Alaska Range. Climbing technically difficult routes during warm weather has been problematic in the past. The warm front made climbing this route hazardous. In this specific instance, the danger from breaking or falling show and ice avalanches was extremely high due to warm weather, suggesting that climbing activity on demanding routes could result in a probable accident. (Source: Eric Martin, Mountaineering Ranger)

HACE, PARTY SEPARATED, FAILURE TO TURN BACK
Alaska, Mount McKinley, West Buttress

Throughout the day on June 17, several expeditions passed Hiroyaki Hoshino (36) and his companions, between 18,000 feet and 19,700 feet. Everyone who passed Hoshino and was later interviewed said that Hoshino looked exhausted and shaky. A ranger patrol descending from the summit stopped to talk to Hoshino and in no uncertain terms tried to convince Hoshino to go down, but were unsuccessful. It is unlikely, but the language barrier could have been a problem in getting the point across to Hoshino.

At the "football field" (19,500 feet) Hoshino was too exhausted to go to the summit. His friends elected to continue and left Hoshino. Hoshino's friends summitted and returned for him. Hoshino had become ataxic from altitude sickness and exhaustion and he needed assistance from his friends to hike down. The Japanese were able to make it down to Denali Pass, where they requested a rescue at 0130 on June 18.

At 0402 the LAMA helicopter and Hudson's Cessna 206 acting as cover plane were in the air to evacuate Hoshino. At approximately the same time, a ground rescue team comprised of volunteers from High Camp was climbing up to assist the Japanese at Denali Pass.

At 0459 the LAMA landed at 18,000 feet, and ranger Kevin Moore assisted the ataxic Hoshino to the helicopter. Hoshino was flown to Base camp where he was treated and stabilized.

Analysis

Hoshino overextended himself. His climbing partners failed to recognize the situation and react to it. Instead they elected to go to the summit. They were also improperly prepared to bivouac, which caused Hoshino to become hypothermic while waiting for a rescue. (Source: Kevin Moore, Mountaineering Ranger)

FALL ON SNOW—UNABLE TO SELF-ARREST, INADEQUATE PROTECTION, POOR POSITION, INEXPERIENCE
Alaska, Ptarmigan Peak, Chugach State Park

On June 29, two instructors and their twelve students in a University of Alaska, Anchorage, Alaska Wilderness Studies 105 Class—Beginning Mountaineering—fell 2,000 feet down the North Couloir of Ptarmigan Peak in the Chugach Mountains near Anchorage. Two of the climbers perished, and 11 of the remaining 12 were seriously injured.

The class hiked to the base of the route on Saturday, June 28. This was the second climbing trip for the twelve novice climbers led by AWS instructors Deb and Ben Greene. They left the tents between 7:00 and 7:30 AM. on June 29 to climb the 2000 foot couloir. All participants reported the ascent went efficiently, albeit slowly. The groups topped out of the couloir at some time between 2:00 and 3:00 PM. Some members of the group hiked to the peak's false summit while others rested. The roped teams reformed, made some adjustments with a few members changing groups and began to descend sometime between 4:00 and 5:00 PM.

On the descent there were again four roped teams with two teams of four and two teams of three. The teams of three had all student members and were placed second and fourth during the descent.

There was a lack of consensus regarding the influence of time pressures on the decision to descend via the couloir. It seems that it was generally understood in the morning that the group would try to be down and back at the parking lot by 5:00 PM, but the relative importance of that goal was interpreted differently by different members of the group. Some considered time to be a major influence on decision making and others, including the instructors, thought it had little to no influence.

Before the class began the descent, there was some informal discussion involving some of the group members regarding the relative merits of descending the couloir versus the walk-off route on the other side. It was decided the walk-off route would be longer and might confront the group with unforeseen challenges as compared to the more familiar couloir.

The first team to descend included instructor Ben Greene (34), with students Jerilyn Pomeroy-Peterson (16), Kirsten Staveland (16) and Jay Chamberlin (28). They were always beneath the other three teams on the mountain. The second roped team to descend included students Juanita Palmer (43), Andrew Murphy (20s) and Steven Brown (23 - deceased). The third roped team to descend consisted of Instructor Deb Greene (38), with students Mona Eben (43), Mary Ellen Fogarty (40 – deceased), and Bernadino Lagasca (33). The top roped team and the last to start the descent had three students, Jacob Franck (18), Eric Schlemme (30) and Joshua Thomas (20).

The members of each rope team were separated from one another by approximately 15-20 feet of rope. All climbers had an ice tool or ax in hand. The four teams had various distances between them and all teams were in sight of each other. The estimated distances between the roped teams varied from 15 to 30 feet at times, with up to 150 feet or more of distance between the bottom team and the top team. At the time of the accident, the teams had descended an estimated 300 to 500 feet down the couloir. Several students and instructors were carrying pickets and flukes but were not placing them for protection. Each rope team was aligned at an angle to the slope with most students using the plunge step as they were descending.

The number of people on each roped team moving simultaneously was directly correlated to the steepness of the couloir and the abilities of each roped team. The instructors modified the descent technique as the couloir steepened and narrowed. Soon after starting the descent, the instructors noticed that some students were having trouble plunge stepping and were falling and either failing to self-arrest or arresting with some difficulty. At the couloir's steepest point, just before the accident, one person on each rope team descended while the other members faced into the slope, bent over their buried ice ax, with their hands gripped around the top of the ice ax. The shaft of the ice ax was plunged into the snow at an appropriate angle to the slope and buried to the top of the shaft. The ice axes averaged 65 to 70 cm in length, although two students reportedly had ice tools that were 50 cm or shorter. The ice axes were attached with leashes to either wrists or harnesses. (Either option was permitted by the instructors.) Unlike the conditions experienced on the ascent, the snow conditions on the descent were described as soft, with each person's boot plunging six to ten inches or more into the snow on the descent. As one climber moved down, the other rope team members faced into the slope in their "anchoring" stance. When the climber in motion reached the end of their rope, he or she faced in, plunged the ice ax into the snow and anchored for the next person to move.

The roped teams descended oriented at an angle to the slope with different distances between each of the teams. There was some bunching of the top teams in the narrow portion of the couloir. Almost from the beginning of the descent until the actual accident occurred, there were several incidents of students slipping and arresting their own fall or someone else on their roped team stopping them.

The immediate mechanism that caused the accident was initiated when Jacob Franck, who was moving down along side teammate Schlemme, slipped and was unable to self-arrest. When Franck's rope went tight, Schlemme was pulled backwards, landing on his back with his ice ax in his hands. Franck and Schlemme attempted to self-arrest but were falling out of control and pulled Thomas backwards so that he also landed on his back with his ice ax in his hands. The secondary mechanism that caused the accident was that the protection/anchoring system failed.

There was an estimated 30 feet of distance between the top team and the next team with instructor Deb Greene. The top team of three climbers fell out of control hitting the next roped team member Mona Eben, who was standing closest to the center of the couloir. She was knocked onto her back with ice ax in hand. At that point Franck, Schlemme, Thomas, and Eben were falling out of control pulling Fogarty, Lagasca and Deb Greene out of their stances and onto their backs. The seven climbers attempted to self-arrest but failing to do so fell into the next team of Murphy, Brown and Palmer. This third team was not moving at the time and were all faced into the slope over their ice axes. When the group of seven entangled climbers struck Murphy, Brown, and Palmer they too were pulled off their stances. The entire group of ten continued out of control down the couloir heading for the bottom team.

The bottom team of Ben Greene, Staveland, Pomeroy, and Chamberlin were able to see and hear the falling teams and, with no time to move, braced themselves for the impact. All four members of the bottom team were pulled off their stances and dragged down the couloir with the other ten climbers in an entanglement of ropes, ice axes and people. (Source: Interviews with participants and instructors, various reports and photographs, and on-site inspection.)

The following information on the ensuing rescue operation was provided by Dr. Ken Zafren, who was the Alaska Mountain Rescue Group Leader.

The accident was observed by three skiers who were approaching the base of the couloir. They were able to reach the victims in about 15 minutes. There were also a number of mountain bikers on the Powerline Pass trail, which passes directly below the base of the couloir. This trail also serves as a utility access road which is closed except to emergency vehicles. The first 9-1-1 call reporting shouts for help came in at 5:10 PM from one of the mountain bikers. When the skiers reached the victims they found the fallen climbers in a ball, some having difficulty breathing because they were entangled in the ropes and others because they were under other climbers. They cut the ropes and moved the climbers off each other as carefully as possible. One of the skiers ran back down to the AWS camp to bring up sleeping bags and to recruit mountain bikers to help.

Although the picture of the accident was still sketchy, by about 5:30 PM, the Alaska Mountain Rescue Group (AMRG) was called along with the Alaska Air National Guard 210th Pararescue Squadron (PJs) to assist the Chugach State Park Rangers and Alaska State Troopers (AST). Anchorage Fire Department Paramedics responded and Anchorage Police closed the road to the trailhead (Glen Alps parking lot) to facilitate emergency access to the incident command area.

While AMRG member Scott Horacek drove up the road, I waited at the Glen Alps parking lot. As Medical Director for AMRG, I would be responsible for initial assessment of the injuries. AMRG member Chris Flowers and I were flown by AST pilot Bob Larsen to a small rock bench, about 150 meters east of the victims. Only a toe-in landing was possible for the Jet Ranger. Chris went ahead while I changed into double boots. It was so warm that I was still wearing just shorts and a t-shirt. I downclimbed the rock bands and sloping ledges which led to the couloir and crossed the hard snow between the landing zone and the victims. We arrived at the site just after 6:00 PM.

The scene that greeted me was surreal. Twelve victims were under sleeping bags and space blankets. There were several skiers and mountain bikers, most dressed very lightly, doing what they could for the victims. Scott arrived from below about the time I reached the site. We did the best we could to start triaging our patients. Loose rock at a steep angle made every movement more difficult. It was hazardous to move above any of the victims, but also unavoidable.

A short time later, the first of two Pavehawk helicopters carrying the PJ's arrived and hovered below the scene. In all, nine PJs were lowered from these helicopters and walked up a short distance to the scene. The PJs carried medical supplies. Two Anchorage Fire Department paramedics arrived by AST helicopter and were assisted by AMRG members to the scene. Eventually, 11 AMRG members were on scene for a total of 33 rescuers, including the bystanders. We required eleven litters and the same number of backboards or vacuum mattresses. All twelve survivors were airlifted by Pavehawk. Eleven were transported directly or via Life-Guard Helicopter to hospital and were admitted. The police Chaplain and The American Red Cross Disaster Unit responded to the command area to provide moral support and food for families and rescuers. A total of 93 persons, including helicopter personnel, were involved in the pre-hospital phase.

There were too many patients for one person to triage, so Master Sgt. Brent Woodiness assisted me as well as handling communications with the helicopters. The helicopters were staged from a flat moraine top near the AWS camp and were able to operate continuously for many hours by use of in-flight refueling from an Air National Guard C-130 which circled overhead to provide air cover. In addition, the trooper helicopter and a contract private helicopter provided continuing air support. The first victim left the scene by 8:30 PM and in four hours, all of the rest were evacuated.

The rescuers picked up debris at and below the scene (much of it blown away and down by rotor wash) and also dismantled the AWS camp. Although the pilots were willing to extract us from the field the way we had arrived, all of us elected to walk to the bottom of the couloir and take off from level ground.

One patient was admitted to the ICU where she stayed for several days. Several underwent emergency surgery for extremity injuries including an open femur fracture and a knee fracture dislocation. There were no internal injuries necessitating surgery nor were there any serious head or spinal injuries.

Analysis
1. Technique. The instructors' decision to use an untested descending technique with no back-up system contributed to the cause of this accident. At first glance it appears that having two or three climbers "anchoring" the rope team while one member descends is a secure method. Had the slope been less steep and snow conditions more favorable (that is firmer), their improvised system might have been sufficient to hold a fall.

It would have had an even greater chance for success if this system had been enhanced by having each climber tie a two-inch diameter loop in the climbing rope two to three feet from the harness. The ice ax shaft would then go through this loop. In this manner, when climbers were in the anchoring stance, the force of a fall would be transmitted to the ax/anchor instead of to the climber's harness.

The mechanism of failure was probably due to the following: When Jacob Franck fell, the next climber on the roped team, Eric Schlemme, was pulled by the rope from behind and below. Schlemme had his toes kicked into the snow, with his upper body pressing downward on the ice ax while gripping the top of the ice ax with both hands. It appears the toes of his boots served as a fulcrum as the downward force of Jacob Franck pulling at Schlemme's waist caused Schlemme to be jerked backward and away from the slope while he instinctively held on to the ax, pulling it from the soft snow. The third member of the roped team, Joshua Thomas described a nearly identical mechanism of failure when Schlemme and Franck pulled him off his stance. When the topmost team slid into the next roped team, it initiated the same sequence of failure that continued until all the teams were in an uncontrolled fall down the couloir. It is significant that nearly everyone interviewed said that they found themselves on their backs with their ax in their hands immediately after they were pulled or knocked from their stance.

In hindsight, the instructors should have elected to use more traditional methods, such as setting their pickets and flukes as fixed protection, or lowering the students from a multi-anchored belay. The safest alternative would have been to descend via the walk off route.

2. Protection. Roped teams on steep snow with no fixed protection contributed to the magnitude of the accident. Roped travel without fixed protection is usually done on the relatively flat surface of a glacier as a precaution for crevasse falls or on uneven terrain where at least one climber can obtain a secure position. On rare occasions a guide may rope to a client without fixed protection when the guide is confident of holding a fall.

It has been observed that climbing teams roped together on steep terrain often have a false perception of security. A high percentage of mountaineering accidents that involve climbing falls share three common factors: (1) descending, (2) roped together and (3) no fixed protection. A rope without fixed anchors invariably becomes the primary mechanism of multiple injuries during a fall.

The descent system lacked redundant safety. (See, for example, previous comment on the ice ax/loop technique.) All mountaineers recognize the need for redundant safety systems while climbing, and in particular while teaching others to climb. Deb and Ben Greene mistakenly thought that the combination of the students being roped together, their newly learned ability to plunge step and self-arrest, and the "anchoring" technique described earlier represented a redundant system. In fact, with no fixed protection, each roped team was dependent upon every person to perform flawlessly. Thus any uncontrolled fall could have resulted in an uncontrolled descent of the entire roped team. Considering the minimal experience the students had, they should not have been relied upon as a critical component of a "safety system."

3. Instruction. Students reported that all instructions that were provided were clear and understood. They carried out the instructions, but were unable to perform the self arrest and belay under the conditions encountered. The next appropriate step in the instructional sequence would have been for the instructors to confine their activities to the lower third of the North Couloir.

4. Position. With only 15 feet between each student, the reaction times for self-arrest are very limited, making it harder to stop a fall before weighting the next climber in line on the rope team. Short roping students is often used in steep snow conditions. However, the more traditional technique involves short roping only the students, leaving a long section of rope between the students and instructor. The instructor then sets a belay and lowers the group of students.

The rope teams were inadvertently stacked above each other creating a "net" like effect and contributed to the magnitude of the accident. The North Couloir's narrow, funnel-like contour made it difficult for the tightly grouped rope teams to stay out of each other's "fall-line" and inevitable that a fall by the uppermost rope team would capture the rope teams positioned lower on the slope.

In situations where rope teams must descend a snow slope, it is imperative each rope team stay clear of the other's fall line. Maneuvering through a narrow chute presents special problems that usually involve groups descending one at a time and clearing the fall line before the next group descends. The lack of a safe run-out contributed to the severity and magnitude of the accident.

5. Supervision. When determining an appropriate ratio of students to instructors, several factors are taken into consideration. These include the terrain, the skills of the participants, and the overall profile of the participants. The relatively large student to instructor ratio of 6:1 seems inappropriately matched to the difficulty of the climb and experience level of the students and may have contributed to the accident. With only two instructors for four rope teams on a steep, narrow couloir, it seems almost inevitable that rope teams would be close together for the sake of communications, and therefore positioning—as indicated—is critical. Additionally, a large group of students in difficult terrain presents an instructor with a significant amount of information to process in a very short period of time. Keeping track of six students in two separate groups, some of whom are falling, scared, or practicing improper technique, would be extremely difficult under the best of circumstances.

It is also important to note that it is inappropriate to allow beginning students to lead and/or to be on a roped team independent of instructors under conditions where the safety of the students would be compromised should a fall occur. (Source: Jed Williamson, Daryl Miller, Jim Ratz—External Review Team)

(Editor's Note: Several recommendations were put forward by the review team in December of 1997, and the University of Alaska, Anchorage, is in the process of implementing these.

Obviously, this was a very high profile event. There was a considerable amount of media attention, some of it quite critical. Part of the concern was around the length of time between the incident and this reviewer's team engaging in an investigation and report. It should be understood that few educational institutions are prepared to respond to a multiple trauma event, so determining what actions are "appropriate and timely" requires significant focus and effort.

This was an extremely difficult situation for all, including the investigators. I was called upon in the fall, and solicited the expertise of Daryl Miller, Mountaineering Ranger from Denali, and Jim Ratz, former NOLS Executive Director. We appreciated the full cooperation of the participants and friends, the University and its Alaska Wilderness Studies program, officials, local guides, and community members.)

FALL ON SNOW, PNEUMOTHORAX
Alaska, Mount McKinley, Karstens' Ridge

Jonathan Giesen's (25) accident happened July 5 at 2200. We summitted the previous day (July 4), arriving back at high camp at 1850. We slept in on the morning of the fifth, relaxed, and prepared to go on a "night schedule" for our descent. We started the descent from high camp (16,800 feet) at 1700 July 5. It had snowed earlier in the day so that our trail to Browne's Tower was covered with a foot of fresh snow. Jonathan was on the trail-breaking team led by Jeff Carter.

After a rest break to retrieve our cache at Browne's Tower, Rob Hess' rope team took over leading and breaking trail down the Coxcomb and Karstens' Ridge. Jeff's rope team followed in second position, with Jeff at the back of the team. Approximately 1.5 feet of new snow covered our tracks on this portion of the route, making footing somewhat tricky but doable, especially with the protection afforded by the fixed line which we installed on the way up. On the last section of the fixed line, Jonathan had the jumar on the fixed rope in his right hand and his ice ax in his left hand. Here he stumbled and somersaulted approximately six feet. The fixed line held him on the relatively gentle slope (< 35 degrees), and he regained his feet, apparently unhurt, and continued 15 feet to the end of the fixed line. He disconnected from the line and continued with the rope team down Karstens'. After 100 more feet, he stopped and bent over, prompting an inquiry from Jeff Carter. Jonathan replied that he couldn't get his breath and thought that he might have "stuck" himself. Jeff instructed the rest of his four-person rope team to stick their ice axes in for anchors, then belayed himself down to Jonathan. He was obviously having a difficult time breathing and upon inspection had a wound in his left side that did not initially appear serious to Jeff. Nevertheless, Jeff dressed the wound with an occlusive dressing. Leaving Jonathan's pack, Jeff got Jonathan to his feet to continue the descent to the camp at 12,200 feet (short-roped). However, as soon as Jonathan stood, his breathing worsened and he was unable to move.

Richard Lewis, a student on one of the following rope teams, is a practicing paramedic. Jeff requested that his rope team pull parallel so that Richard could consult with Jeff about Jonathan's injury. The remaining rope team began to construct a tent platform at a more level spot immediately below the fixed line. After examining the wound, Richard agreed with Jeff that the wound was not immediately life threatening and that Jonathan should be able to move down the mountain. The two of them calmed Jonathan. Jeff traveled behind Jonathan down the ridge and at various points belayed him down steeper sections to camp at 12,200 feet. Jonathan's pack was left behind for others to bring down. Jonathan's breathing moderated during the descent and he was able to move slowly down to camp, where two other roped teams had a tent and hot drinks waiting for him.

Once in the tent, Jonathan was placed in a sleeping bag with hot water bottles and given hot drinks. A more thorough secondary survey was completed, and the wound was cleaned and dressed. Jonathan's breathing became more labored and painful, and he was unable to take a deep breath without pain in his upper left quadrant.

The four instructors and Richard Lewis were concerned about the possibility of a tension pneumothorax, and observed Jonathan closely for signs of such. The weather was clear and calm, with inconsistent cloud cover at approximately 10,000 feet. Evacuation procedures were initiated at 0120 with a cellular phone to NOLS requesting helicopter support. (Source: Jeff Carter, NOLS Instructor)

At 0210, the Talkeetna Ranger Station was notified of the incident by Park Dispatch. The NOLS party had prepared an LZ at the 12,200 foot camp. The Park's contract LAMA helicopter with Pilot Doug Drury and Ranger Roger Robinson departed at 0546. Hudson Air's 206 with pilot Jay Hudson and SCA Doug Demarest departed at 0556 to fly cover for the helicopter. Weather was clear and calm allowing for a direct flight to Karstens' Ridge via the East Buttress. The LAMA landed at 0637 and was back in the air with Giesen at 0644. Giesen was given oxygen in flight and flown straight to Talkeetna.

Upon reaching Talkeetna, Giesen's pulse was 72 and his respirations were shallow at 26. His skin color and condition were normal. An Alaska Air Guard Pavehawk helicopter landed at 0704 and transported Giesen to the Alaska Regional Hospital in Anchorage, where it was determined that Giesen had sustained a pneumothorax.

Analysis
A pneumothorax is a life threatening injury that requires immediate medical attention. The NOLS party made the right decision to evacuate Jonathan Giesen as quickly as possible. This party had excellent communication through the use of a cellular phone and an aircraft radio. Due to their remoteness on the north side of the range, these forms of communication became a real life-saver. (Source: Roger Robinson, Mountaineering Ranger.

(Editor's Note: First, a correction from last year's ANAM in the section on Alaska. On page 17, it was reported that Dennis Gum was experiencing "chain stokes' breathing." That should, of course, read, "Cheyne-Stokes..."

A final note is about a climber from Poland who was issued two Violation Notices upon returning from his climb on Mount McKinley. One was for disposing of food at 11,000 feet, and the other for disposing of fuel, food, and garbage at 14,200 feet. He stated "I was too tired to pack it out, it was so heavy." He did say also that he was sorry for leaving it.

In any case, the business of citations for such things as this and "creating a hazard" has become a part of mountaineering rangers' routine.)

RAPPEL ERROR—ROPE ENDS UNEVEN, FALL ON ROCK, NO HARD HAT
Arizona, Oak Flats
On April 6, following a bouldering contest in the area, Paul (25) and his climbing partner (24) went for a climb about a half mile from the primary bouldering area, where there is some quality granite. Paul had just completed following a single pitch 5.9 route and was preparing to rappel. He was wearing a seat harness. The rope had been doubled so it could be retrieved at the bottom. Apparently, the two rope ends did not meet at the bottom. Within about 30 feet of the top, Paul was rappelling when the remaining strand pulled free. He fell approximately 35–40 feet to the bottom.

An orthopedic physician climbing in the area heard the yells for help and began to assess and stabilize him while someone drove to our rescue camp for help. The rescue team had been breaking down from the rescue/ medical standby at the contest and responded, notifying the local agencies and arriving on scene within minutes.

Paul was unconscious and largely unresponsive the entire time. He was splinted, back boarded, insulated, intubated, and I.V.s were initiated. His breathing had to be assisted with Bag Valve Mask. Due to the terrain and length of evacuation, the team chose to activate the Arizona DPS Ranger 41 from Phoenix early, to perform a short haul extraction (litter and attendant attached via rope underneath the helicopter). Paul was packaged in a

Bauman Bag and extracted with a paramedic rescue team member to a nearby Heli-Spot, where he was turned over to Eagle Air Med and flown to Phoenix, some 70 miles west.

His injuries included a left occipital/parietal skull fracture and concussion, left arm radial, ulnar and wrist fractures, left hip fracture and left leg tibia/fibula and ankle fractures. He was left temporarily unable to speak. Paul was treated and sent to surgery at Phoenix' Maricopa Medical Center, and spent about three weeks in Surgical Intensive Care. Extremely fortunate, he is expected to have near 100% recovery.

Analysis
The rope had been moved by the time of our arrival but was intact. The anchor at the top was reported as intact as was the harness. There was no apparent equipment failure or fracture.

Certainly, this all underscores again the value that companions and bystanders play early in an incident. This mission also would have taken much longer had the team not been in the area, and Short Haul (or cable hoisting) is not an option which is available everywhere or to all public safety agencies. Most areas in the country still do not have rope rescue teams who can comfortably operate in the wilderness. Reporting accurate information, early is critical. It may be the difference between life and death, but more often it is the difference of having some residual pain or discomfort versus having a life long limp or paraplegia or other disability—not being able to climb anymore.
If you are not specific with what you perceive are the technical needs of the mission, local agencies will many times send a local fire department or police officer to "check it out" before activating any technical rescue resources.

The key elements to report to 911 (or your local equivalent) are as follows:
1. Your buddy's condition. Is the person in a life threatening situation? Could he or she survive the night or a lengthy response?
2. Access to the scene. Does there appear to be a road head (for ambulance or truck access) or Heli-Spot (100 feet by 100 feet, no obstructions) at least within 1/4 mile? If not, and your climbing buddy is unconscious or has a serious injury tell 911 that you need a wilderness rescue team with rope skills, and tell them that vehicles or helicopters will not be able to get close. In the game of wilderness rescue, this report, along with minutes, count.

Another consideration is whether it is a fifth class approach or fourth class with severe exposure to access your buddy. If it is, specify the need for a CLIMBING rope rescue team. (Source: Tim Kovacs, Ops Leader, Maricopa County Sheriff's Office Mountain Rescue, Central Arizona Mountain Rescue Association)

(Editor's Note: Tim Kovacs pointed out that an extremely small percentage of our total missions were climbers or mountaineers. The vast majority [99%+] were hikers and other non-climbers who were in over their heads, and for that reason are not reported here.)

EQUIPMENT FAILURE—ASCENDERS CAME OFF ROPE, FALL ON ROCK, INADEQUATE SELF-BELAY
California, Yosemite Valley, El Capitan
On May 27, Robert Jatkowski (30) was cleaning pitch 28 of the Shield, while his partner, Uwe Reissland (38) waited at the belay above.

After finishing a long left-facing vertical corner, Jatkowski reached a Lost Arrow piton about one meter below a roof. From the Lost Arrow the rope ran up and left at 45 degrees to a fixed piton under the roof, a meter left of the corner, then traversed several pieces further left.

Preparing to pass the Lost Arrow and clean it, Jatkowski detached his upper ascender with his right hand, reached up and left with it as far as he could, and clipped it to the rope below the fixed piton. Then he pulled down on the rope below the lower ascender, also with his right hand, and released its cam with his left. His intention was to un-weight that ascender and let rope slide through it until his weight came onto the upper ascender; this would swing him to the left under the fixed piton—a typical move when traversing.

The next thing he knew, both ascenders were off the rope and he was falling. He was not tied in short and was near the top of the pitch, so a long loop of rope hung below him. Most of the fall was free, but his left foot struck a ramp after 10-15 meters. He estimates the total fall-length was 35-40 meters.

After coming to a stop he checked himself, decided he had no serious injuries, re-rigged his ascenders on the rope, and climbed up again. His left foot hurt but he was able to finish cleaning the pitch. He was also able to follow the next pitch, the last on the climb, using only his uninjured leg, but the 2nd class summit slabs brought him to a halt.

Jatkowski waited at the top of the climb while Reissland hiked to the Valley and notified the NPS. Rangers flew to the summit, splinted Jatkowski's leg and helped him hobble 400 meters up the hill to the LZ. At the clinic he was diagnosed with a fractured left ankle.

Analysis
Jatkowski's upper ascender, operated by his right hand, was a right-handed Petzl. The lower one was a left-handed model almost identical to the Petzl, but made in Czechoslovakia. Each ascender was rigged in typical big-wall fashion, with a daisy chain to the harness and an étrier to a foot.

Neither climber saw how the ascenders came off the rope, but it seems unlikely that a correctly attached Petzl—with the safety latch fully engaged—could escape by itself. So Jatkowski probably did not completely reattach the upper ascender—more likely since reaching up and left with his right hand was an awkward move. The spring torque in the cam will usually swing the body of an ascender parallel to the rope by itself, allowing full engagement of the cam and the safety, but tension from the daisy and the étrier can easily prevent this; sometimes just the weight of the slings are enough. In these cases the climber must manually rotate the ascender into position.

Since the ascender was right-handed, the cam, safety, and rope channel now faced toward the rock, away from Jatkowski. He remembers that he did not check the ascender after attaching it, so an incomplete attachment would have been easy to miss. Jatkowski opened the cam on the lower ascender by pushing back on the thumb bar attached to the safety latch. This moves the cam away from the rope, allowing the rope to slide in the channel, but it also begins swinging the safety out of the locked position. If the rope is pressing against the cam at this time it can push the cam all the way open and escape from the device. This is possible with both the Petzl and the Czech model, although the latter seems more prone to it because of the shape of the safety latch.

Jatkowski, Reissland and I rigged a full scale model of the problem on the wall of a building, and I simulated Jatkowski's action while wearing his harness and ascenders as he had rigged them. When I re-attached the upper ascender incompletely to the rope it did not automatically rotate into the locked position, being held back by the daisy and étrier.

It's tempting to assume that we know the answers, but our evidence is really only circumstantial. We do know, however, that Jatkowski would not have fallen so far had he tied in short to his rope (just below the lower ascender) before the traverse. He is very experienced, including on Yosemite walls, and has tied in short in the past, but it just did not occur to him in this case. With the summit only a pitch away, he felt he may have been climbing hastily and not concentrating on the task at hand.

Several injuries and deaths have happened this way in the park, with several models of ascenders (and almost always on traverses). In every case, tying in short would have prevented the accident, and checking the ascender after attaching it would probably have prevented the incident in the first place. (See, for example, ANAM 1987, Schrattner, El Capitan.) (Source: John Dill, NPS Ranger, Yosemite National Park)

EQUIPMENT FAILURE—HOMEMADE RIVET HANGER, FALL ON ROCK
California, Yosemite Valley, El Capitan
On May 29, at 1430, Canadian climber John Chilton (36) started leading the A1 rivet ladder on pitch 24 of the Shield, heading for Chickenhead Ledge. At about the fifth rivet, he placed a homemade rivet hanger (a swagged loop of cable), clipped his étrier to it, and stepped up, leaving his daisy chain attached to the previous rivet, between his knees and his feet. After he had shifted his weight onto the hanger, the cable swag failed. He fell about seven feet and was caught by his daisy.

He immediately felt pain in his lower left rib cage, so severe he had a hard time breathing. He rested in his etriers for an hour and a half, hoping he could climb on, but it hurt to move and he felt a distinct protrusion in his lower chest. His belayer, Rich Prohaska, lowered him to the belay and set up their portaledge to make him more comfortable. Prohaska took the lead, but Chilton's pain was such that he was unable to belay, so they spent the night where they were.

The next day Chilton, though still in considerable pain, belayed Prohaska up to Chickenhead Ledge. He found jumarring too painful so they decided that Prohaska would solo off and go for help.

While Prohaska was fixing pitches another party arrived at the portaledge. They offered to complete the route and get help so Prohaska could care for his buddy, but that night Proshaska and Chilton decided to flash SOS signals to the Valley floor with their headlamps. Eventually they heard rangers calling them by loudspeaker. By blinking their lights in response to the rangers' questions, they were able to describe their problem.

The next morning, the 31st, an NPS team flew to the top of El Cap, lowered two rescuers, and raised Chilton to the summit (leaving Prohaska to jug out with a rescuer). At the Yosemite Medical Clinic he was diagnosed with a fractured rib. They taped it in place and released him (at his request) with a prescription of pain killers and instructions to watch for blood in his urine. It was a couple of weeks before he could walk normally and six or seven weeks before he could climb.

Analysis
Chilton blames his broken rib on the buckle of his harness, a common design with the buckle just left of center. It was of high quality, fit him well, and was properly cinched up, he feels. He'd taken leader falls with it before with no problems. The difference this time was most likely the high stopping force of the daisy.

With his daisy chain still attached to the previous piece, he had set himself up for a fall factor of 1.5 to 2 (depending on slack in the daisy). That's a hard fall that requires a stretchy climbing rope to keep the forces low. Nylon webbing (e.g., Chilton's daisy) is too stiff, and spectra is even worse. In either case you may break yourself or the daisy or rip out the piece.

Often you don't need to clip in the daisy in the first place; it only serves as a keeper for the etriers, but they are already indirectly clipped to the rope. If you do clip the daisy, clip the rope through the piece as soon as your harness is level with it, and disconnect the daisy well before it will interfere with the rope's stretch if you fall—usually before testing the next piece. (Don't forget to allow for slack in the rope.) Some climbers leave the daisy clipped in but rig a Screamer in series with it as a shock absorber. If you do so, make sure the Screamer is designed for the job.

Chilton's injury was relatively minor but could have been fatal. The spleen lies directly behind the lower left ribs; had it been ruptured by the blow or later by the fractured end of the rib, he could have bled to death rapidly. (See ANAM 95, Oliver, El Capitan.) (Source: Martin Ziebell and John Dill, NPS Rangers, Yosemite National Park)

FALL ON ROCK, PROTECTION PULLED OUT, NO HARDHAT
California, Yosemite Valley, Middle Cathedral Rock
On June 16, around 1330, Tyler Gregory (18) started up Pee Pee Pillar, a one-pitch, 5.10a thin crack, belayed by Casey Hyer (19). He scrambled 10 feet up to a ledge, climbed another foot or two, then placed a TCU at arms reach and continued up. At the crux, with the TCU at his feet, he fell off.

"The crack stops and the route goes over a bulge and opens up into a dihedral. I got to the top of the crack and thought there were some holds above that I couldn't see. I tried reaching for them but didn't find anything and that's what initiated the fall."

The TCU pulled out, and Gregory flipped over when his feet struck the ledge on the way down. He landed on the ground on his left shoulder blade and the side of his head after falling 20-30 ft.

Gregory was unconscious for about two minutes; he was convulsing and did not respond to Hyer's calls. Other climbers came over to stand by with Gregory, so Hyer ran to his vehicle and drove to Yosemite Village for help.

The SAR team and the AMR ambulance crew responded immediately. When they got there, Gregory was responsive but complaining of back pain. They gave him oxygen, immobilized him in a vacuum body splint, and carried him 200 yards to the ambulance. About an hour after the accident the AirMed helicopter met them at El Capitan Meadow and flew Gregory to Doctors Medical Center in Modesto.

Analysis
"I had a skull fracture. I was not wearing a helmet on the climb and the doctors said I was really lucky. I was in intensive care for three days and in the step-down unit for another two, but they didn't have to operate or do anything really major. I also had double vision for two or three months and burst my left ear drum. My hearing came back a little bit but the loss is pretty permanent. But I'm climbing again.

"Before the accident I'd been climbing a total of two years and leading traditional routes for about a year, three or four times a week. It was the first climb of the day, hot weather, I felt a little lazy, and that climb is 5.10a, probably at my leading limit.

"So I really didn't feel like doing that climb right then, and I said to Casey, 'It's your turn,' and he said, 'Oh, you'll do it, you'll be fine.' Casey was older than I was and solid on 5.10 and I looked up to him, so there was a lot of pressure on me to not come down from stuff—I didn't want him to think I was a weeny, which is basically stupid.

"I was at the crux thinking, 'I don't want to do this.' But I just gritted my teeth and went for it. It wasn't Casey's fault, but the message is don't let your partner talk you into anything. I tell other partners, 'If you're uncomfortable and you feel like you want to come down, you can come down.'"

The TCU had seemed like a good one, at the time, and Hyer thought that Gregory might have accidently pulled it out by grabbing it as he fell. But that would be difficult to do if he came off with the TCU at his feet. Gregory is competent at placing protection and has fallen on pro quite a bit but, in retrospect, he thinks, the TCU probably failed simply because it was a marginal placement.

That underscores the main message—protection. Regardless of psychology or other factors, Gregory was leading at his limit with one piece protecting him from a serious fall. He places a lot more pro now. (Also see Dular, page 39.) (Source: Tyler Gregory and John Dill, NPS Ranger, Yosemite National Park.)

INADEQUATE WATER, FATIGUE, LOSS OF GEAR, UNABLE TO CONTINUE CLIMBING
California, Yosemite Valley, El Capitan

On July 3, Japanese climber Hideki Inaba (33) began a solo climb of Cosmos (VI 5.9 A4). He had chosen it because he thought it was a beautiful line, a bit harder than he'd climbed to date, and he wanted to climb alone with little chance of meeting another party. (Cosmos gets few ascents.)

The climb is 28 pitches long via the direct finish; an easier but longer option traverses left on Thanksgiving Ledge from the top of pitch 22 to the West Buttress route. Inaba had not decided which way he would go, but he figured he would average 2.5-3 pitches per day. That totaled nine days, not counting four pitches he had fixed. He packed a typical assortment of wall food and 20 liters of water, allowing him two liters per day with two liters extra.

On the 3rd, Inaba climbed his fixed lines and managed one more pitch. On the 4th, he climbed pitch 6 and was fixing the first half of pitch 7 when he saw his portaledge, which had been blowing around in high winds, break loose from its fly and sail into the woods. The twistlock carabiner anchoring the ledge had apparently unclipped itself. He bivouacked back at pitch 5, in slings.

On the 5th he made it through half of pitch 8 (the pendulum was difficult and time-consuming) and slept at pitch 7. On the 6th he bivouacked at the top of pitch 10. This was the first day he had managed over two pitches.

He had hoped fixed gear would speed him along, but he found very little; also the route was brushy (not surprising, given the low traffic), and more awkward than he had expected. Furthermore he was drinking 2.5 liters per day, 25% more than he'd allowed for, so he decided to limit himself to one liter per day. He would climb from 0600 to noon, when the sun first struck the route, and hide in the shade of his fly during the afternoon. Uncomfortable in slings, he was sleeping only an hour each night.

On the 7th, he reached the top of pitch 12 and bivouacked there without fixing. That day he lost his only topo. This worried him because he didn't have the route memorized. He managed two pitches per day on the 8th, 9th, and 10th, taking him to the top of pitch 18. He'd been on the wall eight of his planned nine days and was far behind schedule. Thanksgiving Ledge, where he might be able to ditch some of his gear and take the easier finish, was still four pitches away. Although he had considered rappelling and felt he could do so at any point, he decided to keep going because reversing the traverse and pendu- lum on pitches 7 and 8 would be difficult and he was uneasy about such a long descent.

On the 11th, he started up pitch 19. The first five meters went free, followed by 10 meters of aid in twin cracks. At that point he placed a small camming unit in the left crack and a knife blade in the right. When he weighted them they both pulled, and so did several lower pieces as he fell. He was stopped about five meters above the belay but had fallen upside down and took a blow to the head. He didn't lose consciousness but received a long gash behind his right ear that soaked his helmet with blood. He downclimbed to the belay ledge and stopped for the day.

The pitch had been confusing—especially without his topo—with many ways to go. He seemed physically OK, but being low on water (3-4 liters left), in a hurry to reach Thanksgiving Ledge, and certainly dehydrated, he felt he had not been concentrating well.

Later that day, while adjusting his tent fly, he accidentally knocked his remaining water off the ledge. He had known to clip everything in, especially something as pre- cious as water, and he worried that he might be growing confused. For the first time, he felt despair and thought of rescue. Still, he thought he could continue and did not call for help.

He had also forgotten to clip in his helmet, and that night it, too, fell off the ledge. Whether or not this tipped the balance, he knew he couldn't climb or retreat without more water. At 0600 the next morning, the 12th, he briefly called for help, then sat there for a few hours thinking about his predicament.

Also that morning, Toshiaki Kitajima, an acquaintance of Inaba's, walked the base of the wall hoping to check on him and discovered the bloody helmet. He recognized it immedi- ately and went straight to the NPS with the story. Needless to say, it got our attention!

We soon located Inaba, sitting on the ledge under his fly. With Kitajima translating our questions through a loudspeaker, we were able to determine his situation. By 1130 that morning we were organizing the rescue, but helicopter problems delayed getting our team in place and it was not until 1930 that evening that we were able to raise Inaba to the summit. He spent the night on top with the team and was flown down to the clinic the next morning. He was released after his laceration was cleaned and stitched; deaf- ness in his right ear from the blow to his head was expected to be temporary.

Analysis
Inaba had been climbing for ten years and led 5.9 and A3+. He had climbed K2, Gasherbrum I, and both the Cassin Ridge and West Buttress routes on Denali, as well as the Direct on Half Dome and the South Face of Washington Column. Cosmos was his first solo and first El Cap route.

Inaba found out the hard way that logistics and climbing can be equal challenges on El Cap just as they are on K2. I admire his determination, but, by not accepting that he'd planned inadequately, he put himself in a potentially fatal situation. (Source: John Dill, NPS Ranger, Yosemite National Park)

STRANDED—FORGOT TO UNTIE SAFETY KNOT IN RAPPEL ROPE— JAMMED IN ANCHOR, STRANDED
California, Yosemite Valley, El Capitan
On July 3 Chris Donharl (17), Ben Beezley (17), and Mike Haig (about 25) hauled their bags to Sickle Ledge from the ground but then decided to cancel their climb of the

Nose. They had de-rigged their fixed lines during the ascent, so Mike and Ben rappelled first with the haulbags—four rope lengths on a blank wall east of the climbing route. And Chris followed independently with two ropes and the hardware.

When Chris pulled the ropes after his first rappel, he forgot to untie a safety knot he had tied in the free end of the rope. The knot jammed in the anchor on Sickle Ledge, leaving him stranded at a bolt station in the middle of the face.

Since Chris had most of the hardware, Mike and Ben tried to find other parties who might lend them gear to re-climb the route. When they failed, they decided to contact the NPS.

Two NPS team members began climbing the pitches to Sickle (5.11a) at about 1500. They freed the jammed knot, rappelled to Chris, and all three reached the ground at 1725.

Analysis

Chris and his partners had each been climbing regularly for three to five years, including multi-pitch routes, although only Mike had wall experience.

Crack systems to the west offered a possibility of escape. If he could pendulum to them with his remaining rope he might have been able to make half-rope rappels, leaving gear behind, or possibly solo-aid back to Sickle. However he could not see the cracks very well from his anchor, so he stayed put. The wall was featureless in all other directions and he had no bolt kit.

Chris could have had Mike and Ben fix their ropes on the last rappels as a backup in case something happened to him. He also could have explored the cracks to the west. He could have pendulumed on his remaining 60-m rope, looked the cracks over, and gone back to the bolts if he didn't like what he saw. If he decided to commit to the cracks, he would ultimately have to double his rope so he could pull it. How easy this would be depends on the distance to the cracks, the angle of the face, and his gear and experience.

Another possibility would have been to climb up the jammed rope, hoping the knot would hold. A desperate option, to be used only in the face of otherwise certain death! At least rig some sort of belay to the lower anchor. (Source: John Dill, NPS Ranger, Yosemite National Park.)

FALL ON ROCK, INADEQUATE PROTECTION
California, Yosemite, Half Dome

On July 5, Kibum Lee, Ken Park and I (Jaenam Coe - 35) started a two-day ascent of the Regular Northwest Face of Half-Dome (VI 5.9 A2). Lee, the leader and most experienced member, had climbed several routes on El Capitan and was going to lead all the pitches. I was the least experienced. I'd been climbing three years and had led 5.10 and some shorter aid routes but no big walls. Park and I intended to jumar most of the route and come back to climb it in the future.

We reached Big Sandy Ledge (top of pitch 17) after dark, and the next morning climbed three more pitches to Thank-God Ledge, an exposed 5.9 traverse to the left. Lee and Park belayed at the start of the traverse, but there wasn't room for me so I waited in the corner 10-12 feet below, out of sight.

We knew traverses were tricky, so we had practiced them on short climbs and in a gym. Since I wouldn't be able to watch my partners do this one, we talked about it before Lee started, and agreed that Park and I could follow on Jumars.

Lee led across, placing several pieces along the way. Park followed and anchored my rope, and then I climbed up to the traverse. Thank-God Ledge was about 30 feet long. At the far side the pitch turned straight up for several feet and then left again and out of sight. I couldn't see the belay or my partners, though I could hear them.

At my end, the ledge was a couple of feet wide and looked pretty easy, but part way across it narrowed to a few inches and the main wall got steep. I felt I could make the moves, but Park had cleaned all the protection. The rope stretched across in about the 10 o'clock direction, until it disappeared around a bulge in the face 60 feet away, and I didn't know how much farther it was to the belay. Whether I tried to crawl or walk, belayed by my Jumars, or even if Park belayed me, it seemed impossible to cross without risking a huge swinging fall. I thought Park or Lee should come part way back and place protection for me, but Park was already belaying Lee on the next pitch.

The ledge was separated from the main wall by a crack an inch or two wide, and I had a few camming units. I considered placing them ahead of me and removing them as I passed, but, in my inexperience, I thought they would break or twist out if the pull were sideways to the stem.

I was attached to my rope with my Jumars and with a knot to my harness. That left 10-20 feet of extra rope, with which I thought I could lower myself from the anchor at the start of the traverse. The farther along the arc of the pendulum I could get before I cut loose, the more slowly I would swing, and a ledge, 12-15 feet down and left and about eight inches wide, looked like a better starting point. The wall did not seem overhanging so I thought friction would add some control; however, it curved away, preventing me from seeing what obstacles might lie further left.

I secured a small sling at the fixed anchor, ran the free end of the rope through it and through the figure-eight on my harness, and slowly rappelled with my right hand. My left foot was about three feet away from the lower ledge when I ran out of rope. I thought that if I let go and dropped a bit my foot would touch the lip of the ledge. I hollered at Park and Lee to tell me if it looked O.K., but neither could see me.

I let go. As the rope pulled through the sling, my body swung away from the rock. I missed the ledge and began flying down and left, accelerating as I approached the bottom of the swing. The wall was much steeper than I had thought and there was almost no friction.

I was facing the direction of travel and suddenly realized I was headed for a right-facing corner that I hadn't been able to see from the anchor, fast enough to be hurt if I hit it. I extended both legs horizontally as if to land on it sideways. My feet hit together and I bounced out and around the corner to the end of my swing.

After a few oscillations and trying to slow myself with my feet and hands on the wall, I stopped, 150 feet below the belay. When I looked down, it seemed nothing lay between me and the base of the cliff. I hoped the rope hadn't been damaged on some edge above me.

My ankles were numb, but I did not know I was hurt until I stepped into my etriers to begin jumarring and felt the pain. I managed to get up to Park's anchor, where I wrapped an elastic bandage tightly on the right ankle. I jumarred mostly with my left leg for the next two pitches and my partners essentially hauled me up the last one. By the time I reached the summit I couldn't stand any more and clearly wasn't going anywhere without help.

Earlier, Lee had yelled up to a tourist on the summit to call 911 on his cell phone. Soon the NPS helicopter arrived and I was flown down to the Yosemite clinic. Surprisingly, my left ankle was fractured, not the right one, which was just badly sprained. During the next six months I moved from wheel chair to crutches to various hi-tech splints. Ten months after the accident, I'm walking fine but not yet allowed to climb.

Analysis

Coe was right to be afraid of a pendulum. It's one of the most dangerous falls you can take. If you start, for example, 20 feet horizontally from your pivot point, and strike a corner at the bottom of your swing, you will hit with the same energy you'd have in a vertical fall 20 feet to the ground. The difference is your body's orientation. When you swing, you're more likely to strike your head, chest, and pelvis. Coe was extremely lucky that he saw the corner coming and got his feet up in time. I'll guess that we sometimes fool ourselves because horizontal distance (to a pivot) is not as scary as vertical, to the human eye.

Here are some ways to solve traverse problems. (The best solution will depend on the geometry of the pitch, the security of the protection, the gear available, and, sometimes, whether the moves are aid or free.)

Followers: 1) Let yourself out on a cordalette or a backrope long enough for the job. (You may need the same friction control and safety backups you'd use on a vertical rappel.) 2) Place pro (bombproof!) ahead of you, cleaning it as you go. 3) If you don't have the backrope or the pro, ask the leader to send it down. (Coe could have pulled over the end of a second line tied to his belay line, then used his original line as the backrope.)

Leaders: 1) Think about your partners as you lead. Place protection specifically for them if necessary, and make sure the critical pieces are left in place for the last climber. 2) Shorten the pitch so the angle of swing and/or the radius is acceptable. 3) Rig a second line as a top-rope, direct to the follower instead of through the protection. 4) You have as much responsibility to the follower as your belayer does to you. Don't charge up the next pitch, leaving an inexperienced partner alone to deal with a nasty situation. Be willing to go back to fix it. (Source: Jaenam Coe and John Dill, NPS Ranger, Yosemite National Park)

PROTECTION CAME OUT—FALL ON ROCK
California, Yosemite Valley, Cookie Cliff

On July 14, Darko Dular (33), of Zagreb, Croatia, received fatal injuries in a fall on the Hardd climbing route at Cookie Cliff.

Hardd is a two-pitch free climb, rated 5.11b, that starts from a ledge approximately 10 feet above a rocky, steeply sloping hillside. The first pitch follows the right side of a narrow pillar, 20 feet high, then continues up a hand crack that splits a small roof 30-35 feet above the belay. The climbing is moderate to the roof, but passing the roof involves difficult moves.

With his partner, Elvir Sulich (25), belaying at the base of the route, and the third member of their group, Ivica Matkovich (34), watching, Dular led to the top of the pillar. He stood on the pillar and placed his first piece of protection, a camming device just above his head. This piece was a European four-cam model with a flexible stem and no sling, slightly larger than a #2 Camalot. He did not use a quick-draw with this piece, but clipped the rope directly to it with a carabiner.

Then he climbed higher, placed a #2 Black Diamond Camalot about three feet above the first piece, clipped the rope to it with a four-inch quick-draw, and climbed another three feet or so to the small roof. At that point he decided he did not have the correct protection for the climbing above, so he backed down to the Camalot, intending to hang there while he hauled up the equipment he needed.

He clipped a short sling directly from his harness to the Camalot and leaned back on it. Sulich was not supporting any of Dular's weight with the belay line. Ten to fifteen seconds later, both pieces suddenly pulled out and Dular fell backward. His foot struck the rock pillar as he fell past it, tipping him over. He fell head first through a small tree at the base of the route and into the rocks below the belay ledge, stopping about 20 feet down the slope. The total fall distance was about 50 feet.

While Sulich kept Dular in place with the rope, Matkovich and some nearby climbers ran down to him. He was breathing but unconscious, and bleeding heavily from head wounds. One climber ran ahead 200 yards to his vehicle and drove two miles to the Arch Rock entrance station for help while the rest carried Dular to the road.

NPS rangers, the AMR ambulance, and the AirMed helicopter got Dular to Doctor's Hospital in Modesto two and a half hours after the accident. He remained unconscious, with serious head injuries, for several days, and finally succumbed on July 23.

Analysis

Dular had been climbing regularly for 10-15 years and led 5.12a; he had extensive experience in rock climbing and mountaineering, mostly on European limestone, but also including the Nose on El Capitan, a route on Half Dome, and several other Yosemite routes. Both of his partners were competent climbers. We have no explanation for the Camalot failure, unless a) Dular was satisfied with a marginal placement, or b) he inadvertently grabbed its trigger and released it. This is possible even with all of his weight on the device, though more likely if his weight were partially supported by his feet on the rock.

A properly placed camming device should not fail under the circumstances described by Sulich. While we have no direct evidence, the most likely explanation is that Dular made two inadequate placements. This is hard to understand, however, because he was competent, he seemed cautious and aware of the need for adequate protection, solid placements were available, and he could visually inspect each one.

Should Dular have placed his first protection below the top of the pillar? Climbers say that the placements there are poor and the climbing easy and secure, so they wait to place good protection above the pillar. However, the fact that the landing spot is well below the belay means that the first protection must guard against a serious ground-fall.

Dular was not wearing a helmet. It might not have saved his life, but certainly would have increased his chances. (Source: John Dill, NPS Ranger, Yosemite National Park)

FALL ON ROCK, EXCEEDING ABILITIES, PROTECTION PULLED OUT, INADEQUATE PROTECTION
California, Yosemite, Lembert Dome

I climbed a 5.9 variant of a 5.6 route. I went over the crux successfully, but ran out too far right on 5.6 slope. I place two nuts in marginal cracks. I got to the top of the ledge, then fell and rolled down. I broke a leg and foot.

Analysis

I broke rules. At the top, I put my mid-section over the ledge and reached for a small tree. I let footing leave rocks. The placements were marginal. Poor placement. I was out of sight of belay. Belay saved my life, as did my helmet, because I hit my head enough to cause unconsciousness.

Lesson I learned: 1) Do NOT climb beyond experience level; 2) make all placements BOMB proof before proceeding; 3) do not remove hand or feet from rock, even if you know you "got it made." The climb ain't over until your butt is hooked in on top. (Source: Douglas Hoyt – 48)

WEATHER, INADEQUATE EQUIPMENT
California, Yosemite Valley, El Capitan

On Saturday, November 22, Tim Burnett (26) and Chris Abbott (45) arrived in the Valley for a climb of the Nose. At the Visitor Center the forecast was for clouds but no major storms in the next few days. They asked for an extended forecast, but the ranger helping them got called away and they decided not to wait. They fixed six pitches that day and started up their ropes around 1000 the next morning. They were equipped with waterproof bivy sacks, down sleeping bags, pads, Gortex parkas, waterproof overpants, fleece tops and bottoms, fleece hats, and insulated gloves.

By Monday evening, after two days of great weather, they were bivouacked on El Cap Tower with four pitches fixed above them. They got an early start Tuesday morning under partly cloudy skies, but lost a lot of time waiting for a party ahead of them. They stayed at Camp 5 that night after fixing most of the next pitch, and Abbott set up his bivy on a ledge about 20 feet above Burnett's. At about 1700 it started raining. The party above had pulled well ahead, continued in the rain, and apparently topped out after dark.

Soon it was raining extremely hard and turning to sleet. Burnett was able to stay dry and warm, but Abbott was in a spot where the water drenched him; he was soaked and cold almost immediately. In his 24 years of climbing and mountaineering he had never been in such a storm. The wind shrieked and howled, and the rain pelting their bivy sacks was so loud they could barely communicate to each other.

Eventually Abbott became so miserable that he felt they would not be able to get themselves off the wall. He was sitting up in his bivy sack to avoid the water running down the wall, but was soaked anyway. Burnett suggested that Abbott come down to his more protected ledge, but Abbott declined, afraid that rappelling even 20 feet would be too difficult. Finally, about midnight, without discussing it with Burnett, he started flashing SOS signals with his light.

Burnett was able to stay fairly comfortable for the first part of the night, except that he had to occasionally push himself back up the down-sloping ledge, exposing himself to running water. As time went on, his bivy bag gradually filled and he had to place tennis shoes behind his shoulders and butt to lift himself out of the puddle inside.

At about 0100 Abbott saw a car stop as he was flashing his light. Someone flashed back and the car left, headed toward the village. Forty five minutes later Abbott and Burnett heard a voice hailing them with a loud speaker, but they could not make out the words over the noise of the wind and rain. At one point Abbott thought he heard, "Get to Camp 4. Rescue will start up from the bottom in the morning." [He heard incorrectly.] Eventually the vehicle left.

The rain, snow, and wind continued all night, and they were still socked in at daybreak. They stayed sealed in their sacks for another hour and a half, then decided that no one could rescue them in the existing conditions. Abbott told Burnett that they had to make a run for it by rappelling. When Burnett heard that, "a light went on," and he realized that Abbott was right. They decided that the haul bag with the soaked down bags, pads, and bivy sacks would slow them down, so they threw that gear off the wall, knowing that they were now committed to making it down that day.

At 0730 they started down with their rack, most of their clothing, a copy of the descent topo, their two 60m ropes, and a chunk of rope they'd chopped from their fixed pitch. They warmed up as they rappelled, and their gloves helped a lot, but they were still soaked to the skin. At one point they hung up a rope while trying to pull it, but managed to get it free.

Near Dolt Tower they didn't realize that the descent swings east around a corner, so they continued off route for two or three rappels until they found a fixed rope. By tying their chopped rope to it, they were able to swing east to other fixed ropes leading to the ground (belonging to a party waiting out the storm on Dolt Tower). They now made good time, touching down at mid-day.

The NPS had begun preparing for the rescue immediately after confirming the SOS signals at 0200. We requested the rescue helicopter from Naval Air Station Lemoore, but air operations were questionable given the weather, so a large team prepared to hike (8 miles) to the summit. We canceled our efforts once we were sure that Abbott and Burnett would make it down, nevertheless, gearing up the team to that level required 45 people and the Navy helicopter.

Analysis

A friend with lots of El Cap experience had advised Abbott and Burnett that any precipitation in November would be snow, so they decided down sleeping bags would be OK. However, they had also read "Staying Alive," the safety article in the Yosemite climbing guide, that warns of cold rainstorms throughout the winter and clearly describes conditions on the walls in such weather and the inadequacy of down bags. It also stresses the importance of a rain fly, which Abbott and Burnett lacked.

Experience in the last few years has shown us that plastic sheets and even portaledge flies with bivy sacks are not completely reliable on rock ledges. There are too many ways for water to creep in, especially if you wind up in a bad spot. Although it's a hassle to take along, a portaledge with a properly seam-sealed fly in good condition is your best bet.)

The next best option is to get the hell out of there, but Abbott and Burnett had few defenses if anything went wrong on the descent: 1) They were already wet to the bone, with no storm protection. 2) They had no spare rope and got one stuck, but luckily freed it. (Hint: They could have taken their third rope along instead of chopping it, if, noticing the threatening weather, they had rigged their fixed pitch as a rappel.) 3) Finally, they got off route but stumbled across a fixed line that saved them. (Source: Dan Horner and John Dill, NPS Rangers, Yosemite National Park)

(Editor's Note: There were six climbing accidents reported from Joshua Tree National Park. Five were falls, including a climber who rappelled off the end of the rope. The five were exacerbated by the fact the protection was inadequate. The injuries to all were fractures, including a fractured skull as a result of no hard hat.)

HANDHOLD CAME OFF—FAILURE TO TEST HOLD, FALL ON ROCK, PROTECTION PULLED OUT, INATTENTION
Colorado, Rocky Mountain National Park, Lumpy Ridge

On March 2, Hayner Brooks (44) was climbing with Ken Miller on the route Three's Company (I, 5.7), pitches one and two, into the final (third) pitch of the Thunder

Buttress Route (II, 5.7+) on Thunder Buttress, Lumpy Ridge. On the third and final pitch, Brooks was swiftly leading lower fifth class rock near the top of the formation when a right handhold broke. Brooks plummeted 60 feet down the rock face, pulling one piece of protection—a #3 TriCam—and impacting four times. Miller's belay caught Brooks when he reached his next protection, a #1 Wild Country Friend. As a result of the impacts, Brooks fractured his pelvis on his left side. His chief complaint at the time of the injury was intense pain in the left leg from his buttocks to his toes, and a complete loss of mobility and motion with the left leg. Miller lowered Brooks back to the belay, anchored him, and went down to get RMNP rescue, returning with the team to assist his partner.

Analysis
Brooks and Miller were both experienced climbers. Brooks had been climbing for about ten years, and led rock consistently at the 5.10 to 5.11 level. He had extensive experience on Lumpy Ridge. Brooks blamed his accident on carelessness and inattention, and said that he was moving too fast on the easy rock with thoughts of topping out on the climb foremost in his mind. He did not test the failed handhold, but instead had instantly weighted it, causing him to lose balance when that hold broke loose.

Brooks was wearing a helmet, and attributed this to a lack of any kind of head injuries or loss of consciousness, despite striking his head during the fall. (Source: Jim Detterline, Longs Peak Supervisory Climbing Ranger)

FALL ON ROCK—BLOWN OFF BY WIND GUST, INADEQUATE PROTECTION and PARTNER STRANDED—INEXPERIENCE
Colorado, Rocky Mountain National Park, Petit Grepon
On July 2, Todd Marshall (34) was leading the seventh pitch of Petit Grepon South Face (III, 5.8). At 1900, Marshall topped out on the spur ledge below the summit, stood up with arms upraised, and gave a, "Hurray," and got blown off by a strong gust of wind from the southeast estimated at 60-70 mph by his partner, Matteo Baceda. Marshall fell 70 feet and struck the rock face, sustaining a massive depressed occipital skull fracture, and instant death. Baceda was unfamiliar with self-rescue techniques and remained trapped on his belay ledge 80 feet below Marshall. Baceda sustained exposure to his lips from being stuck out overnight. Baceda was rescued by two climbers during the following afternoon.

Analysis
Marshall, with six years of climbing experience and a prior ascent of Petit Grepon South Face, was the leader of this team and led every pitch. This party was out so late in the day because Marshall and Baceda, during their pre-dawn approach from the Glacier Gorge trailhead, took a wrong turn in the dark and ended up at the base of Spearhead, approximately seven miles away from the Grepon. Marshall was climbing quickly and strongly while leading the Grepon, but he took a 30 foot runout from his last protection, a #2 Camalot, which held his fall. The strong erratic winds encountered were not a surprise to Marshall and Baceda, who had witnessed similar winds all day. Turning back is an option, but at the very least Marshall should have clipped into the belay before standing up on the ledge. Marshall was not wearing a helmet, and the impact area on the back of his head would have been covered. However, considering the distance fallen and the force produced, it is not clear if he could have survived. (Source: Jim Detterline, Longs Peak Supervisory Climbing Ranger)

STRANDED, EXCEEDING ABILITIES, INADEQUATE EQUIPMENT
Colorado, Rocky Mountain National Park, Longs Peak
On July 25, at 0100, David Gallegos and his brother George (26) left from Covenant
Height's Camp to climb Kiener's Route (III, AI 1, 5.4) on the East Face of Longs Peak.
George had climbed the route previously and was to show David the way. They did not
have any ropes, ice axes, gloves, or rain gear. Both men were clothed in all cotton, and
had strap-on crampons which they wore over cloth boots. After ascending Lamb's Slide
and crossing Broadway Ledge, George Gallegos became confused and mistook the North
Couloir for Kiener's Route. When part way up the North Couloir (AI 3, 5.5), George was
unable to continue because of unsteady footing in the snow. The two called for help for
about 45 minutes, after which David continued to the top and down the Keyhole Route,
where he borrowed a cell phone to call 911. Three climbers and later two RMNP rescue
climbers assisted George Gallegos back to the base of the East Face of Longs Peak.

Analysis
The Gallegos brothers had insufficient experience and inadequate equipment for an
East Face climb on Longs Peak. Unroped falls from both Kiener's Route and the Notch
Couloir have occurred in the past and resulted in fatalities. Unroped falls and ascents
without adequate snow/ice equipment have also resulted in injuries and fatalities on
Lambs' Slide. George Gallegos had been rescued previously in a similar incident on
Mount Evans. (Source: Jim Detterline, Longs Peak Supervisory Climbing Ranger)

FALL ON SNOW, CLIMBING ALONE AND UNROPED, EXCEEDING
ABILITIES
Colorado, Rocky Mountain National Park, Mount Meeker
On August 14, Scot Eden (25) was injured while attempting to descend from a partial
ascent of Left Gully (a.k.a. Dream Weaver—II, AI 2), on Mount Meeker. Eden had
turned around on the route when bad weather began building. While downclimbing the
steep snowfield at the base of the route, he slipped and was unable to self-arrest with his
ice ax. He slid 200 feet down the snow, went over a 15-20 foot rock band, and then
tumbled another 100 feet. Eden sustained a fractured right tibia and soft tissue injuries
to the left orbital area of his face. Eden then crawled a quarter mile over the next six
hours until two climbers heard his calls for help. The climbers stabilized Eden with a
sleeping bag and hiked out to notify Rocky Mountain National Park Rescue Team for
the evacuation.

Analysis
Although the Left Gully is an easy to moderate snow climb, it becomes icy in mid-
summer and demands respect. Scot Eden was only moderately experienced at most in
snow and ice climbing techniques, and he obviously learned about the risks of solo climbing on this accident. Downclimbing snow and ice is always more difficult than ascending. Three points of contact with the snow/ice need to be maintained at all times when
downclimbing, and often you have to consciously remind yourself to go more slowly and
deliberately. Mistakes on icy slopes must be corrected immediately or corrections may
become impossible. Falls with crampons often result in ankle injuries, as it is difficult to
keep crampons from snagging on something while falling.
    There are alternatives to downclimbing in case of retreat on Left Gully. From the

notch behind the Flying Buttress where Left and Right Gullies come together, one may rappel one long or two short rope lengths to a ledge system, which is then followed out toward the left. One could also rappel icy sections of the Left Gully on rock or by cutting bollards for anchors on the ice. The final snowfield where this accident occurred may also be skirted to the south on scree. (Source: Jim Detterline, Longs Peak Supervisory Climbing Ranger)

FALL ON SNOW, INADEQUATE EQUIPMENT, NO BELAY, EXCEEDING ABILITIES
Colorado, South Maroon Peak

On August 16, Aspen climber Hillary Trish (21) fell while descending from a successful climb of 14,156-foot South Maroon Peak. Trish fell in clear, warm weather at mid afternoon while attempting to descend the top of the southeast couloir. She was climbing in light hikers without crampons, facing outward and using an ice ax. She was wearing a helmet. The couloir is full of snow year-round and, at the top, rises to a 50 degree angle. Trish fell forward and tumbled approximately 400 vertical feet on snow and rock before coming to rest on a small mud ledge in the south side of the east-facing couloir, around 12,850 feet.

Her fall was witnessed by another climber on nearby Pyramid Peak, who was able to make a scratchy and barely comprehensible cell phone call to the Pitkin County Sheriff. A two-man hasty team was dispatched from Aspen at 1545 to try to assess whether an accident had indeed occurred.

Trish was attended to by one of her climbing partners, an EMT, while her second partner descended another 2,500 feet to a valley floor trail for help. Both the second partner and the initial RP (who made the cell phone call) met the hasty team on the valley trail at 1650. The hasty team continued to climb and reached the victim and her partner at 2100.

On initial assessment, both subjects were suffering from early stages of hypothermia, despite clear, calm weather. They were situated on an east-facing, sloping, mud-covered ledge about 12 by 3 feet, with loose rock on one side and a ten-foot drop into the bergschrund along the side of the couloir's snow on the other. The snow wall rose up about five feet above them.

Trish was A&O x O and combative, with respirations of 28, an uneven carotid pulse of 48 and no evident radial pulse, probably due to cold. She was not responsive, but would talk gibberish every few minutes. Eyes did not track, but pupils were responsive to light. Her partner reported she had been in and out of consciousness. She had a bruise between her eyes and dried blood from her nose. When first encountered she was sitting in her partner's lap. He was holding her to keep her from falling into the bergschrund, which she would have done because of the way she struggled.

The team managed, with some difficulty, to get her into a sleeping bag and onto a Thermarest, then to heat water and place hot water bottles and heat packs around her in the bag. This caused her to calm down and sleep for much of the night. Medical control advised allowing her to sleep, since there was no ability to alter her care if her situation deteriorated.

An attempt the following morning to lower gear from an Army National Guard helicopter was aborted because of rockfall hazard. During two attempts to lower a haul bag from a side winch on a Blackhawk, the bag began to swing, knocking large rocks off the ledges above the party. Rotor wash carried fist sized rocks into the group. Subsequently, a second team reached the first at 0800 the following morning. The victim was packaged, again with difficulty, in a Kendricks Extrication Device and then a Sked, and lowered on a snow lowering system about 1,200 vertical feet to an LZ. The initial slope was 47 degrees. The lowering was complicated by the presence of deep, wide runnels in the summer snow, some as deep as five feet.

The victim was flown out at 1330. She suffered fractures of the pelvis, spine, shoulder and skull, although none required surgery. She later reported that she did not remember the fall or any of the following ten days.

Analysis
One of Trish's climbing partners, her boyfriend, had introduced her to climbing on snow the season before, with an assault on nearby—and easier—Castle Peak. He indicated that they had practiced some self-arrest at the time. However, the southeast couloir of South Maroon is a significantly harder route, and one with significant hazards. The fact that Trish was descending a 50 degree slope without crampons, and while facing out, suggests that she may have been in terrain beyond her abilities at the time of the accident. Her fall, however, carried her to the inside bend of the couloir—which curves right, south, where she landed—rather than into the rock wall on the outside. Additionally, her other climbing partner provided excellent field care and assessment, keeping her stable and in one place for six hours before the first team arrived, and helping through the night. The limitations of the working environment, and the inability to move more personnel up the peak safely in the dark, or insert matériel by helicopter, meant that much of Trish's survival can be attributed to the stable nature of her injuries and her own durable constitution. Had her medical condition deteriorated during the night, no reasonable effort to evacuate her more quickly could have been made. (Source: Hal Clifford, Mountain Rescue—Aspen, Inc.)

HANDHOLD CAME LOOSE, FALL ON ROCK
Colorado, Capitol Peak
On August 17, while approaching the summit of 14,130 foot Capitol Peak along the Knife Edge (the standard route), a 36-year old male mountaineer from Denver fell an estimated 1,000 feet down to a cirque on the eastern side of the peak. The fall was reported about 1030 by another climber with a radio. The victim's body was spotted later that day by a search plane and recovered by a team inserted by helicopter. He had died of massive trauma from the fall.

Analysis
Capitol Peak is one of the more solid peaks in the Elk Mountains, comprised of basalt rather than the loose, sedimentary rock typical of the Maroon Bells and Pyramid Peak. However, the approaches to the summit are extremely exposed on all sides. The victim's climbing partners indicated that a hold had broken loose when the victim grabbed it, and that he had no chance for recovery. (Source: Hal Clifford, Mountain Rescue—Aspen, Inc.)

(Editor's Note: The Knife Edge is a place where climbers of all abilities commonly rope up.)

HANDHOLD CAME OFF—FAILURE TO TEST HOLD, FALL ON ROCK
Colorado, Rocky Mountain National Park, Longs Peak
On August 19, prior to 0900, Steve Mestdagh (39) was leading the North Chimney (II, 5.6) on the East Face of Longs Peak when he dislodged a large rock which he was using for a handhold. The rock gave way as he pulled it. It fell on his foot. Mestdagh sustained severe crushing injuries, including numerous fractures, to his foot. He was able to belay himself off the route to the Mills Glacier, where other climbers assisted him until rescue personnel arrived.

Analysis
The North Chimney is notorious for loose rock problems. When climbing loose rock, one should tap holds to listen for sounds of less-than-solid connections to the rock face, and then gradually weight holds. Another technique useful for survival on rotten rock is to consciously spread out weight over multiple points of contact, pushing in instead of pulling, as is efficiently demonstrated by stemming maneuvers. Also, it's a good idea to budget more time for climbing rotten rock carefully. (Source: Jim Detterline, Longs Peak Supervisory Climbing Ranger)

FALL ON SNOW—UNABLE TO SELF-ARREST, CLIMBING UNROPED, EXCEEDING ABILITIES
Colorado, Rocky Mountain National Park, Longs Peak
On October 11, Madrone Coopwood (24) slid 200 feet on Lamb's Slide at Longs Peak. Coopwood struck the rocks at the base of the snow, sustaining a right illiac fracture, slight rib fractures, and a pneumothorax of the right lung.

Analysis
Studying the past history of a route may allow one to prepare against recurrent problems. Since the epic first slide of Rev. Elkanah Lamb in 1871, Lamb's Slide has been the scene of numerous similar accidents, some even resulting in death. (Source: Jim Detterline, Longs Peak Supervisory Climbing Ranger)

FALL ON ROCK, FAILURE TO FOLLOW ROUTE, WEATHER, PROTECTION PULLED OUT
Colorado, Rocky Mountain National Park, Longs Peak
On October 11, Chris Sproul (26) and David Sweedler (37) began the Notch Couloir (III, AI 3, 5.5) on the East Face of Longs Peak. Sproul and Sweedler gained the top of the Notch feature at 13,900 feet, but then encountered extreme winds and blizzard-like conditions coming out of the West. They decided to traverse along the base of the palisades at the top of the East Face to stay out of the wind, and then top out on Kiener's Route. Once atop Kiener's Route, they intended to traverse below the summit to the descent route for the North Face, which would enable them to stay clear of the main force of the wind and storm. However, when they got to the base of the "Open Book" feature on Kiener's Route, they were unable to figure out the route (go right, up, and over the infamous "Diamond Step") and became stranded in the storm without overnight supplies. At one point, Sproul attempted to climb up the "Open Book," but fell, pulling all anchors but one. Both he and Sweedler damaged their helmets and sustained

minor head injuries. Late on October 13, Sproul figured out the "Diamond Step" and climbed out to get help for his partner. Early on October 14, Sweedler was rescued by the RMNP rescue team. Both Sproul and Sweedler sustained serious frostbite to hands, feet, and face, and may lose some fingers and toes.

Analysis
The nasty first-storm-of-winter that hit Sproul and Sweedler was exactly on time as predicted. Less ambitious plans would have prevented this epic. This misadventure seems to repeat itself every Autumn. The ability to route-find as a mountaineer (the "Diamond Step" is only third class) is more critical to success on the big mountain than is the ability to force a straight line, a strong trait among many pure rock climbers. Despite any judgment errors on the part of Sproul and Sweedler, they should certainly be commended for their will and strength to survive. (Source: Jim Detterline, Longs Peak Supervisory Climbing Ranger)

FALL ON ICE, INADEQUATE BELAY, EXCEEDING ABILITIES
Colorado, Rocky Mountain National Park, Thatchtop
On November 6, at 1300, Chris Chierello (29) was leading the Snake Route (I, WI 4) on Thatchtop North Face, and was belayed by Mark Keating (21). Chierello was leading the final headwall section about 100 feet above the ground, when his tool and crampon placements failed in thin ice, causing him to fall onto a regular (29 cm) Black Diamond tubular screw. Keating was not watching the leader and was not tied into any ground anchors. Keating was yanked upward, wrenching his shoulder at such an angle as to cause a dislocation. Due to the extra rope lost from the inattentive belayer, Chierello fell approximately 30 feet fracturing his right ankle. Chierello was then lowered by his belayer to the ground. Nearby ice climbers assisted Chierello and Keating with their injuries, and ran out to Bear Lake to alert the Park Service. Both climbers were evacuated on plastic snow litters by park rescue.

Analysis
The Snake Route is typical of many winter water ice climbs in that the more dramatic-looking sections, in this case near the base of the route, are often less dangerous than transition areas near the tops of the climbs. Paying attention to changes in ice quality indicates that it may be appropriate to place one last solid screw before venturing into unstable territory. When climbing thin ice, the climber's weight should be evenly distributed among all four points of contact. All new placements should be gradually weighted before being trusted. The belayer, as well as the climber, needs to be tuned in to these changes as well. Thin ice climbs should be practiced under the controlled conditions of top-roped ascents before a leader attempts to lead routes of this nature. Chris Chierello had been climbing ice for two years and only recently began to lead ice. Mark Keating was a newcomer to ice climbing but had experience rock climbing. Both climbers were wearing helmets and plastic boots, which may have prevented additional injuries.

The local emergency room physician reported that he had been seeing numerous injuries to Thatchtop North Face (a.k.a. "The Loch") ice climbers, mostly beginners, of several per week during this winter season. These accidents were not reported to the National Park Service, although required, and so additional helpful tips which may have been gained by investigators are not available. Thatchtop North Face ice has become increasingly popular, with over 25 parties per weekend day observed during winter 1997–98. (Source: Jim Detterline, Longs Peak Supervisory Climbing Ranger)

(Editor's Note: The last observation is consistent with the comment on the cover photograph. Fifty to 75 climbers per weekend can be an estimate close to 1,000 ice climbers for the season)

FALL ON ICE, EQUIPMENT FAILURE—CARABINER, FALL ON ICE
Colorado, Vail, Rigid Inseminator

On December 7, Jim Amidon (31) and Joe Crotty (30), both experienced ice climbers, set out to ice climb in the Designator area. Around 2:00 PM Jim Amidon fell 85 feet from the Rigid Inseminator (WI 5, M7) pulling one ice piton and screw, and snapping a carabiner before decking out. He sustained multiple displaced fractures of the upper femur, fractures of the pelvis, and facial lacerations.

Rigid Inseminator is roughly 90 feet high. The difficulties begin right off the ground. You dry tool up 10 feet, clip a bolt then traverse left horizontally 12 feet making it to the second bolt and a "lousy" stance/rest on a ledge. From here you move up and left to the ice. The initial ice section is a 30 foot vertical sheet, which when combined with the dry tooling start, presents the true crux of the route. Once through this difficult ice section, the angle relents for 40 feet or so until a final steep section bars passage to the anchor.

Joe made the first attempt successfully negotiating the opening mixed traverse and clipping the first two bolts. Upon reaching the hanging curtain Joe felt tired and opted to lower off. Jim, being more experienced, stood a better chance—especially since he had led the same climb in good style with no falls or "hangs" six days prior.

Near the top of the climb, Jim was traversing over thin (1") sloping ice to the anchors about four feet to his right when his right crampon popped off the ice. The ice his tools were in was too thin to hold the additional load and gave out precipitating a fall. The first piece of gear to blow was a Spectre, about six feet below. Eight feet below that was a 17cm screw buried to the head and angled in the direction of anticipated fall. It pulled out completely. The next screw about ten feet below the previous screw held, but the 'biner at the rope end broke sending Jim all the way to the ground. Just before impact a 22cm screw (roughly 18 feet below the screw with the broken carabiner) placed in the direction of anticipated fall caught some of Jim's weight just before impact. Before hitting the ground Jim ricocheted off a small hanging curtain near the base, snapping it off, and the (10 feet high, 3 feet wide, 2 feet thick) ice landed on him as he hit the ground.

Four climbers around the corner on the Rigid Designator heard the ensuing clamor. Luckily, all of them had medical experience and helped get Jim in a stable position and assess his condition. A cell phone call was placed immediately. Vail Valley Fire Department, Vail Search and Rescue, and Vail Valley Medical Center all provided an immense amount of care and manpower to ensure a smooth and safe rescue. Although the approach was only a twenty-minute walk up, it took 31 rescuers three hours to get him out.

Analysis

Jim says he tried to place one more screw above the Spectre, fearing the Spectre was not placed well, but dropped his last screw while placing it. All the protection was intact and only the broken 'biner and the Spectre were damaged. The Spectre was bent from a side load and the 'biner broke at the bottom.

The broken 'biner was two weeks old, bent-gate style and hadn't been used before. Chris Harmston, Quality Assurance Manager from Black Diamond, determined that there was no indication that the 'biner was defective in any way and it just broke from overloading. Chris agreed to inspect the "biner as he is investigating gear failures; the 'biner was not a Black Diamond product. Jim was climbing on two ropes: 9.8mm 60m and 8.5mm 60m. The former had been fallen on once in a year of use and the latter was a brand new two-month old rope with no falls. Pulling out the two upper pieces caused the ropes to be more statically loaded, leaving no dynamic "give" on the 'biner that broke. Both ropes were clipped into the 'biner that failed. The conclusion is that the carabiner failed with the gate open. Be aware that carabiners can, and on rare occasion *will*, break regardless of previous use.

Further, Jim's helmet saved his life. Having witnessed the fall and impact, I can only conclude that Jim would be dead without it. I was further protected by my helmet when Jim's fall created all sorts of blunt flying hard icy objects that hit my helmet. Just the other day I spied a fairly famous ice climber in a trendy magazine eschewing his helmet on an ice nasty. Don't be fooled! Helmets save lives, period. Those suave characters foregoing helmets, especially on ice climbs, are just corpses waiting to happen. (Source: Submitted by Jim Amidon and Joe Crotty)

FALL ON SNOW—UNABLE TO SELF ARREST, CLIMBING UNROPED, NO HARD HAT
Montana, Glacier National park, Rainbow Peak
On July 3, Mark Robison (24) and Christopher Foster (23) fell 2000 feet to their deaths. They had nearly summitted Rainbow Peak when the lead climber apparently lost his footing, taking the second climber down with him as he fell out of control down the narrow, rock-filled snow/ice couloir. The slope of this couloir is approximately 60 degrees.

Analysis
It took some time to find these overdue climbers, who were known to the rangers because they worked on the trail crew. Robison and Foster were very fit and experienced and prepared for the route they had elected. They had previously accomplished such feats as a fifty mile "day hike." The route they had chosen was a long one, which is perhaps why they chose not to rope up. Neither climber was wearing a helmet, and no fixed protection was used. There was not enough evidence to indicate exactly what happened to initiate the fall, nor to indicate which of the two was in the lead. (Source: Scott Emmerich, Supervisory Resource Management Ranger)

RAPPEL FAILURE—ROPES TOO SHORT, STRANDED
Nevada, Red Rocks Canyon NCA
On February 8, the Las Vegas Metropolitan Police Department SAR unit responded to a call regarding a stranded climber on a rock face at Willow Springs. The victim (25) was rappelling when he realized his rope was too short. He had tied himself off about six feet from the end of the ropes—about 50 feet above the valley floor.

Two officers got above him, anchored a rope and lowered it to him, advising him to tie off and remain there until rescuers came. As the rescue team was getting organized, the victim self-rescued on the rope lowered to him, using a double carabiner brake.

Analysis
The victim was fortunate enough to realize his mistake before rappelling off the end of his rope, on which he had not tied a knot. He also had the presence of mind to tie himself off and then use a carabiner brake system. However, luck was on his side in trusting to a line dropped by strangers, the line tied only to an anchor of unknown origin, and without communicating to the people tending it. (Source: James Roberts. Las Vegas Metropolitan Police Department SAR)

FALLING ROCK
Nevada, Red Rocks Canyon NCA
On May 2, on the fifth pitch of the Original Route (5.9,A2) on the Rainbow Wall in Red Rock Canyon, a climber (35) accidentally dislodged a four foot by two foot by six inch sandstone block that fell 100 feet before striking his partner (34)on the back of his head and back. The two then rappelled to the base of the route, where the victim was placed in his sleeping bag and his partner left to find help. The Las Vegas Metropolitan Police Department SAR unit responded, and the victim was successfully evacuated by litter and helicopter. In addition to the injuries to his head, he had a tension pneumothorax.

Analysis
Loose rock is common on many of the routes here, even the ones that experience a lot of traffic. The victim's helmet was deeply scored, and given the laceration on his scalp under the helmet and the size and force of the falling block, he almost certainly would have been killed had he not been wearing a helmet.

Being able to self-rescue to the bottom of the route, even though the victim was not able to walk out, made a reasonably timely rescue possible. It may have prevented the victim from becoming hypothermic or developing a life threatening tension pneumothorax during the course of what would have been a complex night time big wall rescue. (Source: James Roberts, Las Vegas Metropolitan Police Department SAR)

(Editor's Note: Two other accidents were reported from this area. One involved a hiker [65] who found himself in a climbing situation, desperately stranded as a result of separating from his partners without telling them. He was located and flown to safety. The other victim was a novice ice climber who was " bouldering" on ice while his partner prepared to climb. The victim fell ten feet, fracturing his leg. A cell phone contact with the rescue team probably prevented hypothermia, but, as they noted, cellular phones cannot take the place of good judgment.)

FALL ON ROCK, INADEQUATE PROTECTION, INADEQUATE BELAY
New Hampshire, Whitehorse Ledge, Standard Route
In July, a father of unknown age and his 14-year-old son were climbing Standard Route on Whitehorse Ledge. The father was leading the crux layback corner, and the son was belaying at Lunch Ledge. It is reported that the son was not belaying properly and other climbers reminded the boy to "hold the rope." It was also witnessed that the father looked like he was having difficulty climbing the 5.7 crux, and his protection may have suffered as a result. The father fell while on the crux and hit the slab below suffering an angulated open fracture of the right ankle and fracture of the left ankle. Whether his belay failed or protection failed is unknown.

When the fall occurred, Mountain Rescue member Ian Turnbull was at the foot of the cliff and by the time he climbed to Lunch Ledge, climbers at the scene had the father lowered back to Lunch Ledge. Ian rappelled with the father on his back one rope-length to a two-bolt anchor on the slabs below. A second rescuer arrived to help by lowering Ian and the injured father to the ground by tying ropes together and passing the two knots.

Analysis
The father hadn't been climbing for ten years, and it is apparent that the son was not fully competent in his belaying. I do not know the exact nature of the fall and why the injuries were so severe. The rock in that section of the climb offers many easy protection possibilities, and a leader need not subject himself to a dangerous fall. I can only speculate that the leader either placed poor protection that failed, or did not place enough protection. There is also the possibility that the leader's protection was fine and that he just landed badly on a relatively short fall on a slab that is not very steep. The crux he fell from is nearly vertical for 10 to 15 feet, but the slab he landed on is less than 45 degrees. There is a subtle art to falling (landing actually) and ideally a good leader tries to realize when he might fall and prepare for the landing.

The rescue went smoothly except for a knot jamming in a Gri-Gri during the knot pass on the long lower. Tying ropes together and lowering on a single strand is a great rescue technique, but the knot pass can be a problem if you're not prepared. One technique is to let a releasable friction hitch take the load from the lowering device before the knot jams. With the system backed up to the anchor, pass the knot and release the friction hitch. (Sources: Mountain Rescue Service, Inc)

FALL ON ROCK
New Hampshire, Cathedral Ledge, Recompense
A party of two climbed Recompense, and the leader fell while on the crux third pitch. He fell 10 to 15 feet and hit a ledge, badly breaking his leg. The climbers had the experience and knowledge to initiate their own rescue. The belayer was able to get the leader back to the belay and set up a lower on a single rope strand to get the leader to the ground. When New Hampshire Mountain Rescue and local paramedics arrived, they had only to put the leader into a litter and carry him out.

Analysis
The crux on the last pitch of Recompense is technically a 5.9; however, the layback moves on fingertip holds are very strenuous. Protection is very good if you can hang on long enough to place it. One suggestion is to climb up, get the protection in place and in that spot it is easy to step back down to a good rest, recover, then continue climbing.

It is good to see climbers self sufficient enough to rescue themselves. In this case their method worked and was quick. The patient really suffered as he was being lowered down the cliff, bumping into the rock on the way down. We could hear his screaming as we approached the cliff. It is possible that a better method would have been for the uninjured climber to counter balance rappel with the patient to keep him away from the cliff. (Source: Mountain Rescue Service, Inc)

FALL ON ROCK, PROTECTION FAILED, LOOSE ROCK
New Hampshire, Cannon Cliff, Whitney-Gilman

On October 29, Daniel Becker (19) and Jonathan Waldman (19) were switching leads on a very crowded Whitney-Gilman with multiple parties above and below. The party immediately ahead of Daniel and Jonathan were having a difficult time on the crux, the infamous "pipe pitch". The steep and intimidating pipe pitch goes out right over the imposing north wall before veering left again onto the southeast face. Having had to retreat in the past due to crowds, Daniel saw a possible variation on the cliff that would hopefully allow them to pass the bottleneck on the pipe pitch. He was hoping to climb straight up and meet the normal route again at the end of the pitch. Starting from the belay at the end of the second pitch, Daniel climbed up a little and found a fixed piton, which he clipped as protection. Knowing the piton was of questionable security, he soon placed a camming unit in a crack which turned out to be the back of a refrigerator-sized block. He also placed a stopper in a crack that he knew was a poor placement, but trusted the camming unit just below. Climbing ten feet higher, he stopped to look for more protection when his foothold broke and he fell. The stopper failed and the camming unit began to arrest his fall, when the forces the cams placed on the rock became greater than the forces that held the rock on the cliff. The refrigerator-sized rock broke free, and Daniel was falling again. His belayer Jonathan described feeling the belay working. He could feel that he was stopping Daniel's fall when all pull on the belay just stopped. This was the point when the big rock broke free. Luckily for Daniel and the parties below, the rock fell off to the left causing no harm. Daniel was tumbling and landed face first on a flat ledge breaking his jaw, nose and fracturing his skull. He continued to fall, but the pitons in a corner on the second pitch held, and he came to a stop hanging from his rope about 20 feet below and to the right of Jonathan. The total length of his fall was 60 to 70 feet.

The climbing party below, Dr. Josh Boverman and Christian Caslin initiated the rescue. Boverman used a cell telephone to call 911 at 11:48 am and NH Fish & Game was notified. A separate climber identified only as "Jay" lowered Dr. Boverman to Daniel while Caslin maintained contact with Fish & Game. Boverman assessed Daniel's condition and the two were lowered to a ledge. From this ledge on the first pitch, they lowered Daniel to the ground. Dr. Boverman felt that Daniel's conditions could be life threatening and that he needed immediate medical care beyond what could be done at the foot of a cliff. Daniel had been unconscious for a period of time, but had regained consciousness by now.

Eight Fish and Game officers arrived on the scene by 1:00 pm and called for a National Guard Helicopter. Many climbers on the scene were able to help lower Daniel in a litter down the talus, away from the cliff where the helicopter was able to pick him up at 3:35 pm. He was flown to Littleton and then to Dartmouth-Hitchcock Medical center in Lebanon.

Analysis
Both climbers were experienced, and Daniel had climbed the route before. One could criticize Daniel and Jonathan for climbing below other parties on a route famous for big loose rocks, however that did not directly contribute to the accident. Daniel's problem was that he either misjudged the structural integrity of the crack where he placed the cam or misjudged the ability of the camming unit to subject the rock to such high forces. As protection, camming units are able to hold a fall when placed in a parallel crack by

pushing out against the crack more than they are pulled down by the falling climber. A climber can develop high forces in a fall, and the dynamic climbing rope will absorb most of this, but as much as 2600 lbs. can remain in the system. The remaining force is roughly doubled where the rope passes through the protection doing the catching; this is approximately 5000 lbs at the protection! The cams need to push out more than the 5000 lbs. is pulling them down in order to remain in the rock. This is a severe example, and Daniel's fall could not have resulted in such high forces but evidently it was enough to get the large rock to break free. Good protection is more than the hardware staying in the rock, it's also the rock staying on the cliff! (Sources: Jonathan Waldman, Daniel Becker, and other climbers on the scene)

(Editor's Note: Jonathan has recovered and is climbing again.)

AVALANCHE
New Hampshire, Mount Washington, King Ravine

King Ravine is a large glacial cirque located in the Northern Presidential Range. It features several prominent avalanche paths and starting zones. There are no avalanche forecasts issued for this part of the range.

On November 23, Joël Reigner and Luc Parent were ascending the Great Gully Trail, a steep and difficult hiking trail (and major avalanche path) in King Ravine. On a round-trip day hike, they carried crampons, ice ax, day packs and headlamps, but no avalanche rescue equipment. While they did know something about avalanches, they assumed it was too early to be a concern.

As they ascended the trail, they triggered numerous small avalanches. Although they had no formal avalanche training, they were able to recognize the instability but considered the small avalanches inconsequential. They proceeded up towards tree line, slogging through thigh deep pockets of wind deposited snow as the trail became increasingly steep. At this time, Joel and Luc had separated to about 15 to 25 feet apart. Luc, who was trailing behind, became concerned about the possibility of a larger avalanche and made an effort to move to the right of the gully where the snow was shallower. Luc attempted to tell Joel, who was climbing in the middle of the gully where the snow was much deeper, to also move to the right but the distance between them made communication difficult. It was now dark, and Joel's headlamp had failed. At approximately 5:00 pm, Joel triggered an avalanche that swept him down the gully.

By Joel's approximation, the avalanche was a soft slab with a crown 10 feet wide and 4 to 6 inches deep. The slide ran 150 feet and carried Joel past Luc, safe on the right of the gully. Fortunately for Joel, the snow came to a stop on a bench, preventing him from being carried over several small cliffs to the floor of the ravine. He estimates his burial depth of three to four feet. Joel was buried on his left side, with his head and right arm above the snow. He yelled out, and could see Luc's headlamp above him on the trail. Luc thought he heard someone yelling, but dismissed it as his imagination. Luc thought it was too dangerous to descend the trail to look for Joel. Both the steepness of the trail and the possibility of starting another avalanche intimidated him. Later, during the interview, he affirmed his awareness that successful avalanche rescue must be carried out by the victim's party. Nonetheless, he continued up the Great Gully Trail in hopes of finding the Spur Trail. He intended to hike to the Grey Knob cabin to report the accident there.

In the meantime, Joel was busy digging himself out of the avalanche. His mouth and nose had been filled with snow. Still clutching his ice ax in his right hand, he used it to dig the snow out from around himself. After 40 to 50 minutes of self-excavation, Joel set out to find Luc. He continued up toward tree line, became lost without his headlamp, dug a snow-cave, and settled in for a long cold night.

Luc was lost. His headlamp died as well and he was forced to bivouac. On the following morning, Luc was unable to find the trail and bushwhacked his way down to the ravine floor, walked out and reported the accident at a local fire station around 11:30 am, 18 hours after the accident occurred. A rescue team was dispatched and as the advance party began hiking, Joel appeared at the trailhead. He was cold, tired, had a large bruise on his leg and a twisted ankle.

Analysis
It is obvious that both men are very lucky to escape unharmed. Not only did they survive an avalanche, but also the notoriously dangerous winter weather of the Presidential Range had been fairly mild for spending an unprepared night out above tree line. It is worth repeating that successful avalanche rescue must be carried out by the victim's party. US Statistics show that a victim completely buried has only a 20% survival rate after 30 minutes. (Source: Kai-Uwe Allen, Snow Ranger, US Forest Service)

VARIOUS FALLS ON ROCK and INADEQUATE PROTECTION, RAPPEL ERROR, DISLODGED ROCK
New York, Mohonk Preserve, Shawangunks
Of the sixteen accidents related to climbing in this popular, easily accessed area, we have a typical profile for the majority of cases. There were fifteen falls, in which seven resulted in protection coming out. There was one rappel error in which the rope ends were 40-50 feet apart. The resulting fall, fortunately, resulted in no injury. The average difficulty of the climbs on which the accidents occurred was 5.66, and the average age of the climbers directly involved was 36.8.

The most interesting accident involved a seasoned 'Gunks climber (59) who engaged in a deliberate leader fall on High Exposure (5.6) for a filming crew. Some protection pulled, and he fell backwards, hitting his back and head.

Interesting injuries included a climber who impaled his hand on a carabiner, a bruised belayer whose partner had fallen on him, and a rope burn that occurred when a climber grabbed the rope running to his belayer after he fell. (Source: From the report submitted by the Mohonk Preserve and Jed Williamson)

FALL ON ICE, PROTECTION PULLED OUT, EXCEEDING ABILITIES
North Carolina, Doughton Park
On January 19, Shawn Hansen (30) died after the anchors he was using to support his friend on an ice floe broke loose.

Hansen's friend, Ed Williams (30) of Raleigh was climbing up the ice floe at Ice Rocks, a popular ice climbing area in Doughton Park, when he fell off the ice, apparently causing the anchors attached to Hansen to give way. Hansen fell about 80 feet, hit ice and rocks, then rolled another 70 feet down the rocky slope. Hansen was dead when rescue crews arrived on the scene at 10:55 a.m. Williams fell to the base of the slope, but the rope slowed his fall and he was not injured.

Hansen and Williams had been rock climbing together for about four years, but they were fairly inexperienced ice climbers. (Source: "News and Observer," Raleigh, NC, January 20, 1997).

(Editor's Note: Aram Attarian, who helps collect data from North Carolina, indicates that this is the second fatality from ice climbing in ten years.)

FALL ON SNOW—FAULTY USE OF CRAMPONS
Oregon, Mount Hood, South Side
On April 4, a climber (32) was glissading below Crater Rock when his crampons snagged on hard snow, resulting in a fractured tibia. (Source: Jeff Sheetz, Portland Mountain Rescue)

(Editor's Note: Perhaps we should put New Hampshire guide George Hurley's mantra on all crampons: "There is no good reason for glissading with sharp spikes on our feet."

FALL ON SNOW, CLIMBING ALONE AND UNROPED
Oregon, Mount Hood
On May 19, Carlos Loria (age unknown) was descending the Coe Glacier after making the summit. He slipped and fell 700 feet, fracturing his neck. He had been reported overdue by his brother. Rescuers found him, noting lacerations on his face, slight hypothermia and the cervical injury. He was helicoptered to Portland.

He had been accompanied by his dog, Buckwheat, but the dog was not in evidence. A month later, the dog appeared at the Cooper Spur Inn. He had apparently survived on snowmelt and berries. As the newspaper reporter said, "Too bad Buckwheat can't fill us in." (Source: Hood River County Sheriff's Office and "The Oregonian," June 25, 1997)

FALL ON ROCK, EQUALIZED SLING FAILURE
Oregon, Smith Rock State Park
On June 7, a climber was being lowered by his partner after climbing the route, Easy Reader (5.6) at the Dihedrals in Smith Rock State Park.

After descending about 15 feet, the anchor sling failed sending the climber free falling approximately 60 feet. He landed on his feet, hip, arm and body in that order, and suffered numerous fractures.

Other climbers in his group provided immediate care until EMT's from the Redmond Fire Department arrived. About 45 minutes after the accident, he was evacuated by helicopter to a Bend, Oregon hospital.

Analysis
After the evacuation, two climbers climbed an adjacent route to inspect the anchor system. A locked carabiner remained in each hanger, and a locked and regular carabiner were on the rope. From this it was concluded that the single, equalized sling failed for some reason. The lead climber had set up the anchor system and then rappelled down to belay the climber. For climbers that had considered an equalizing sling bombproof, the accident came as a shock.

Cause of the failure has not been determined. Two climbers independently inspected the remaining slings in the leader's pack and found all solid water knots. The sling had carried the rappel load, but then failed with approximately 80% more weight. Tensile tests were carried out on slings with knots that were intentionally not dressed (twisted or folded), but these performed surprisingly near to perfectly tied knots.

One possibility was that the knot did not take a set, and slipped through to the melted end on rappel, and continued slipping on the victim. Regardless of reason for failure, it is strongly recommended that setting a single sling, equalized or not, should only be done after careful deliberation as to the risk. It is recommended that any anchor system with bolts or gear be set with two independent, bombproof anchors, or at least three good independent anchors by traditional gear placement. Bombproof means two modern solid anchor bolts with hangers, solid horns or trees.

Independent slings or quickdraws should be clipped to each anchor point to provide sufficient back-up for an individual sling or anchor point failure. If one judges the need for an equalized sling, it should be backed up with the rope or slings slightly longer to allow equalized movement) to each anchor point. (Source: Michael Dianich)

FALL ON HARD SNOW—CRAMPONS ICED UP, UNABLE TO SELF-ARREST
Oregon, Mount Hood, Palmer Glacier
On June 11, Andy March (32) was descending from the summit of Mount Hood about noon when his crampons became "iced up," and he was unable to clear them by tapping them with his ice ax. He slipped and fell 300 feet before he was able to stop his fall.

His partner summoned help at Timberline Lodge, and a rescue team proceeded to help March down the mountain. They returned to the lodge by 7:30 p.m. March was transported to Mount Hood Medical Center for an evaluation of his chief complaint—lower back pain. (Source: Clackamas County Sheriff's Office)

(*Editor's Note: The term "iced up" most likely means consolidated snow that did not dislodge using the usual method of tapping—or giving a good whack—with one's ice ax. Experienced climbers like these fellows would not use an anchored belay in this kind of situation, but those with moderate or less experience should.*)

FALL ON SNOW, CLIMBING UNROPED, SNOW CONDITIONS—NÉVÉ
Oregon, Mount Hood, Cooper Spur
On September 6, Mark Fraas (40) fell 1500 feet down the Cooper Spur after losing his footing.

Analysis
There have been at least 13 fatalities on the Cooper Spur. All follow a similar scenario: loss of footing, inability to self-arrest, and a long fall over rock cliffs above the Eliot Glacier. Because of the hazardous fall line, this route should only be attempted when snow conditions give firm footing and the party is prepared for immediate self-arrest. These conditions are usually present in the very early hours of spring mornings.

Friends of Mark Fraas indicated that he had climbed Mount Adams and Mount

Hood several times, that he was an expert telemark skier, and that he was not a fool-hardy person. He and his partner, Rodney Brenneman, were carrying skis and were not trying to reach the summit.

It was also reported that he was a person who "did everything to the limit." Further, "He was always ebullient, enthusiastic... operating at a different level than most people." (Source: Jeff Sheetz, Portland Mountain Rescue; and "The Oregonian," September 8, 1997).

Excerpts from a letter by Rodney Brenneman, Fraas' partner, to the Crag Rats Mountain Rescue offered the following:

I feel there are three likely potential causes of Mark's fall: One, he was hit by a rock and knocked off balance. While he wasn't wearing a helmet, there was almost no rock-fall and this seems highly unlikely. Two, his crampons lost grip or edge points broke out. I found no icy or crusty spots at all, nor was the snow the slightest bit slushy (I was wearing gloves with no shell, placing my one hand against the snow constantly, and my gloves weren't the slightest bit wet). This is possible, but seems less likely than the third possibility: He caught his crampon points (probably left foot) on his leggings as he stepped through. This I believe is the most likely cause. Mark was wearing leg warmers he had made, which could be pulled down to boot top (like cyclists use) if they become too warm. He had these pulled down (as well as his sleeves off) at the time of the fall. Given the steepness of the slope, there would be a very small space for the uphill leg stepping through during traversing.

Regardless of the cause, the fact that Mark was traversing (*piolet canne*) without anchoring his ax meant any slip was a fall. Finally, once he lost his ax (and without a leash to perhaps help him retain it) there was no chance of arrest. I also have no idea how familiar he was with self-arrest techniques.

I understand from others that Mark was an excellent and experienced telemark skier. Nothing I know or heard about Mark indicates that he had any experience as a "climber"—except in the context of doing approaches for skiing. I have climbed and taught rock climbing for a number of years, and climb grade WI 4 ice. Mark had the knowledge of the local terrain, fitness and confidence of an experienced "climber." In retrospect, it is my gut feeling that he may not have had the experience to judge when he had crossed over his technical limitations and when to adopt a more conservative approach.

Cooper Spur should never be climbed fourth class—roped but without placing pro-tection. You don't stand a chance of holding another climber's fall on this steep a slope without some anchor. I don't feel unroped climbing is unnecessarily dangerous for an experienced climber on this route—as it is the fastest method of ascent. Personally, the only change I would have made would have been to use two axes in *piolet panne* (with leashes) so that I always had an anchor. It is just as fast and is safer. There is a danger with two axes and leashes should you somehow come off, however. I believe that self arrest is nearly impossible from the upper slope in the *névé* conditions we had and that the climber must not fall.

In conclusion, I think information which alerts people to the seriousness of the Coo-per Spur route is one of the best accident prevention tools. The most dangerous aspect of the Cooper Spur route is that it never really looks or feels dangerous or particularly exposed—at least until one is very committed to the upper portion.

FALL ON SNOW, FAILURE TO FOLLOW ROUTE, INADEQUATE EQUIP-MENT, EXCEEDING ABILITIES
Oregon, Three-Fingered Jack, South Ridge

On October 26, Karl Iwen (20s) fell to his death while descending Three-Fingered Jack.

As he was unfamiliar with the mountain, Karl asked to join two climbers he met at the trailhead. They completed the "technical" part of the climb (ascending and descending) then unroped to hike out. There was a patch of snow covering rock west of the climber's trail, and Karl ventured out onto this snow. He slipped and could not stop his fall. The other two climbers watched Karl, but were unable to help him. He carried an ice ax, but it was strapped to his pack at the time of the fall. He slid into a couloir and dropped about 600 feet in a tumbling fall.

Analysis

Karl was not familiar with the mountain and the route, but left his companions and did not follow the climber's trail off the mountain. Also, venturing out onto snow above the west face of the mountain with his ice ax strapped to his pack showed a lack of awareness of the dangers he faced in this alpine environment. Karl had just moved to Oregon from the Midwest. (Source: Jeff Sheetz, Portland Mountain Rescue)

(Editor's Note: The other three accidents from Oregon included AMS brought on by fatigue, occurring at the 11,000 foot level on Mount Hood; a fractured ankle incurred upon jumping over a crevasse on Mount Hood; and a fractured heel after a 15 foot fall on Mount Washington's West Ridge. There was a telemark skiing injury below Crater Rock on Mount Hood. He fell several times, ultimately attributing this to having his skis on the wrong feet!)

FALL ON ROCK, RAPPEL ERROR, DARKNESS
Utah, Zion National Park, Prodigal Son

On New Years, 1997, John Christensen (36) died while soloing Prodigal Son in Zion National Park. Having fixed two pitches the previous day, he tried to complete the route in one push on December 31, New Year's Eve. I last saw him climbing by headlamp at 9 pm. I was bivied on the seventh pitch of the Lowe Route.

Analysis

Judging from the speed he was climbing, it seems that he would have made it to the top. But for some reason, at night, he rappelled the route. The SAR team recovered his body January 2. (His watch had stopped at 1:34 am.) The SAR team believes that because he was rappelling on ropes of different diameter (7mm and 10.5 mm), he rappelled off the end of the thin rope after it slipped. But no one is sure.

He should not have rappelled. If he made it to the top, he should have walked off. There is a paved descent trail which takes one hour to walk down. If he did not make it to the top, it's highly probable he made it to the bivy at the base of the last pitch. Perhaps he couldn't free climb the sparsely protected 5.4 section in the dark. Then he should have bivied. There is a large dirt ledge (you can unrope) and trees and bushes for protection. It was cold, but above freezing, so he would have survived. He was climbing with full rain and cold weather gear.

Soloing is not to blame, although if he had had a partner, perhaps something would have been double checked.

This is the first climbing fatality in Zion National Park. There have been two previous deaths in Zion involving rappelling, but these from canyoneers, and were not considered to be "climbing" accidents by the Park. (Source: Dan Stih)

AVALANCHE
Utah, Provo Canyon, Bridal Veil Falls

A large, out-of-the-ordinary storm struck Utah on January 25. It snowed heavily along the Wasatch Front until noon and then switched to a mixture of heavy rain and snow, and later in the afternoon went back to snowing. Ice climbers were on the ice in the vicinity of Bridal Veil Falls during this warming period. The Bridal Veil Falls area in Provo Canyon is world renowned for spectacular ice climbing and it is also the location of the steepest tram in the world. That was until last year when the tram was destroyed by an avalanche.

About 1215, an avalanche came down through a chute just east of Bridal Veil Falls. It caught two roped together ice climbers, swept them off the ledge they were on and took them 250 feet down steep terrain through scattered pines and oak brush.

Other ice climbers in the vicinity responded. One of the victims was buried in about two feet of snow and they said the rope made it easy finding him. They called the Utah County Sheriff's Office on a cell phone while they were digging the victim out. They said that one victim was seriously hurt and that they were doing CPR on a second victim.

Members of the Utah County Sheriff's SAR were immediately dispatched and arrived in under an hour. An avalanche dog and a handler from nearby Sundance Ski Resort also responded in case there were other victims. The ice climbing area is about 800 feet above the canyon floor. The steep ascent combined with knee-deep snow in pines and oak brush made the climb difficult. An attempt was made to stay clear of the avalanche runout zones, but there were not many choices in getting to the victims.

The approaching hasty team was split. Three members went to the injured victim and two to the possible fatality. The injured climber who had been buried was Scott Lee from Sandy, Utah. There is no doubt that the ice climbers saved his life. Scott knew his climbing partner, Doug Hall, was probably dead.

Scott was still caught in a pocket of rock-hard avalanche debris. It was not easy to get him out of the hole and onto a backboard. His injuries included hip, lower back and chest pain, and the whole side of his head was starting to swell. Scott said he broke his back skiing the year before and that this accident might end his winter sports.

Scott's vital signs were stable and his level of consciousness good, but he was shivering uncontrollably and he was soaking wet. Everyone agreed that the best course of action was to stabilize him and go. As he was being packaged in the stokes, an avalanche ran out of Lost Canyon, across the highway from the rescue. It came down at least 2000 feet and it stopped at the edge of the highway. The billowing snow cloud came halfway across the canyon and it was an awesome sight. The command post had the canyon closed. The weather conditions were letting up some, but the blowing rain and snow continued. Scott, the rescuers, and the belay system rope were soaking wet and caked in ice.

Scott was delivered to waiting Provo Paramedics and Doug Hall's body was brought out twenty minutes later. As everyone was driving out of the canyon, another small avalanche ran just west of Bridal Veil Falls. It was good to be out of there!

I checked with the Utah Valley Regional Medical Center the following morning, and Scott was listed in stable condition with internal injuries. (Source: Chris Reed, SAR Team)

FALL ON ROCK
Utah, Diamond Fork

On May 8, we were paged out at 1730 for a fall victim, still hanging from his rope, in Diamond Fork Canyon.

When I arrived on scene the boy (victim) was sitting in a car. Dick asked me to check him out, but the boy did not want any medical attention. He had been up walking around prior to deputies arriving on the scene.

The boy's father requested that he be transported by ambulance to the hospital to be evaluated. Dick asked me to check his injuries. I put a cervical collar on him. He had a laceration to the top of his head, but no other obvious injuries. He was aware of time and place, and I had difficulty in convincing him to stop moving his neck and back. He just kept moving his neck, twisting and reaching over to the other side of the car, after I told him numerous times to stop moving his head and back.

His companions, a guy and two girls, were quite concerned about his well being and one of the girls was quite emotional. She had run down the road to Little Diamond when she was unable to start the injured boy's car.

I talked to the boy who was teaching them to rappel. He said that he was on belay as well as on the rappelling line. That was fortunate. The injured boy had not yet started rappelling when he lost his balance and tumbled over the edge. Since he was on belay, he did not fall very far, but he pendulumed and struck his head. His companions said he lost consciousness and was hanging limp in his seat harness. They said he even had some seizure activity. The one girl ran for help while the others lowered the injured boy to the ground. He regained consciousness and was able to walk down to the road and their car.

Spanish Fork Ambulance transported him to Mountain View Hospital. (Source: Chris Reed, SAR Team)

FALL ON ROCK, FATIGUE, MISCOMMUNICATION
Washington, Icicle Creek, Eight Mile Buttress

On Sunday, April 16, Andy Tonning was participating in a rock climbing field trip as a student in the Seattle Mountaineers Intermediate Climbing Course. He was ascending the Tree Route on Eight Mile Buttress. This is a popular multi-pitch route which has been used by climbers for decades and is rated 5.6 or 5.7. The first pitch of the route may be started on the left as a chimney rated 5.6 or 5.5 or may be started on the right at a steep crack rated 5.7. Sam LeBarron was Andy's instructor and was belaying him at the time of the fall. Three other students and one instructor were ahead of Andy and Sam on the route. Two of these had completed the first pitch, and the second rope team was on the pitch, followed by Andy, who was leading.

The climber who was climbing just ahead of Andy was having difficulty because he was wearing a heavy pack which seemed to be pulling him over backward and made it difficult for him to complete some of the harder moves. Andy, now on the route, waited behind this climber while he worked to overcome the difficulty.

In the meantime, two other climbers who were not in the course arrived at the base of the route, accompanied by their two dogs. Another instructor, Vera Dewey, was also at the base of the route, observing.

The climber ahead of Andy gave up on the 5.7 crack and moved to the easier chimney. At this point, Andy had been waiting 15 to 30 minutes at a resting point. He then started up the crack. He had difficulty at the crux of the crack, and spent longer than he felt he should getting through the move. As a result, he grew tired and felt that he should either down-climb to the resting point or hang from the rope to rest. Andy decided to use his remaining strength to add a piece of protection and then hang his weight on the rope to rest and shake out his tired arms prior to continuing the climb.

After adding the piece of protection, Andy felt that his strength was almost gone, so he called, "Falling," three times, waiting approximately five seconds between each call. He did not call out his belayer's name in conjunction with yelling, "Falling." Vera, who could see Andy, heard a call of "Falling" and directed Sam to "take up the slack." Sam immediately began to take in some rope. At that time, Andy "released from the rock" for a short rest. The remaining slack in the system, together with normal rope stretch was sufficient to allow Andy to fall approximately ten to twelve feet onto a shelf before the rope grew taut enough to stop his fall. All of his protection held securely. Sam was not pulled tight against his anchor, and no rope slipped through his belay device.

Sam lowered Andy to a safe place. Andy had swelling in his right ankle, which was subsequently bandaged by Vera. Andy decided he could walk to the trailhead with assistance. He then drove to Seattle on his own where he was diagnosed with a fractured fifth metatarsal in several places, a hairline fracture of the ankle and a small chip to the outside ankle.

Analysis
Several factors may have contributed to his accident, but predominately, it was one of poor communication between climber and belayer. Calling the belayer's name along with, "Falling," might have helped reestablish communication. Also, Andy might have avoided the fall if he tested the system before committing his weight to it, or clipped directly into his protection. (Source: From a report written by a panel of five members of the Seattle Mountaineers and written statements from party members)

FALL ON ROCK, LOOSE ROCK
Washington, Tumwater Buttress
On Sunday, April 26, Linda Olson was participating in a rock climbing field trip as a student in the Seattle Mountaineers Intermediate Climbing Course. She was leading the second pitch of Tumwater Buttress. Linda climbed to the top of a short pillar and reached the crux of the climb, which was a bulge formed by several large flakes of rock. She placed a wired stopper while standing on top of the pillar then proceeded to work her way up the flakes. She suddenly yelled and was falling, with a large rock falling with her. She fell past her belayer. After she landed, the large flake struck her leg and then her arm. The fall was estimated to be around 25 feet. Her belayer (John Wick) and another rope team provided first aid. Linda sustained a broken arm and broken leg.

Analysis
The wired stopper pulled out during the fall, but it is unclear whether this made a difference in the outcome. Linda was wearing a helmet, without which her injuries would have been much more serious. (Source: From a report written by a panel of five members of the Seattle Mountaineers and written statements from party members)

ACUTE MOUNTAIN SICKNESS, MISCOMMUNICATION, INEXPERIENCE
Washington, Mount Rainier
Mount Rainier communications received a radio call on May 21 from a team of three climber/researchers in the summit crater of Mount Rainier. The reporting party, Francois LeGuern leader of a French research team, indicated that one of his members was suffering from Acute Mountain Sickness (AMS). LeGuern reported that Eric Bouvet, exhibited the signs and symptoms of vomiting, insomnia and general malaise with an increase in severity over the last 24 hours. Bouvet was part of a film crew documenting volcanic research.

LeGuern's team spent the previous four days on the summit conducting research and sleeping in the steam caves. During this time, a storm deposited a significant amount of snow on the upper mountain creating an increased avalanche danger. Due to the avalanche hazard and Bouvet's condition, it was decided to evacuate the team from the summit by helicopter.

Approximately 90 minutes after initial contact with LeGuern's team, NPS rangers Kirschner, Gauthier, Yelverton, and Carney were flown to the summit in a military Chinook helicopter. Bouvet was assisted from the research cave, across the crater and into the helicopter. Bouvet was then flown to Madigan Army hospital for evaluation and treatment.

Analysis
LeGuern's party was part of a larger 15 member research and film team, some of whom had limited climbing experience. The team had spent two days acclimatizing at 11,000 feet prior to ascending, but Bouvet still suffered from the effects of altitude on the summit, perhaps due to the extended time spent there. It was later determined that Bouvet felt sick prior to ascending but told no one because he thought it was due to the food he ate. Additionally, the snow storm had created an increased avalanche hazard, estimated at moderate to high, preventing the research team from safely descending on their own. Since AMS can lead to further complications and is considered life threatening if untreated, flying Bouvet during the break in the weather was the best option for his safety.

Climbers on Mount Rainier may feel the effects of altitude but extended acclimatization is generally not required. Most climbs take two days and climbers descend back to sea level before many of the serious symptoms arise. Acclimatization is very difficult because most climbers come from sea-level. Parties that expect to stay at altitude should have a systematic plan of acclimatization. Better communication among party members is stressed, especially with those less experienced who may confuse an upset stomach with AMS. (Source: Mike Gauthier, SAR Ranger, Mount Rainier National Park)

STRANDED, INADEQUATE FOOD and FUEL
Washington, Mount Rainier, Liberty Ridge
On June 15, two climbers called on a cell phone to the White River Ranger Station to report that they were pinned down in bad weather on Liberty Cap. Mike Catlett and Don Willcox had successfully climbed Liberty Ridge under favorable weather conditions but were caught in a lenticular cloud once they reached the summit. Unable to find the descent route due to reduced visibility, high winds and accumulating snow, the climbers decided to set up camp and wait out the bad weather. They also indicated that they were low on food, fuel and water and expressed concern about their situation but did not indicate the need for rescue or help.

Conditions remained poor on the upper mountain for the next 24 hours. The party again called White River Ranger Station on June 16 to report that they were out of food and nearly out of fuel. They felt the situation was not urgent, however they believed that they would not be ambulatory if they had to go another day in similar conditions. The weather forecast called for continued high winds and cloudy conditions for the next two days.

On June 17, a ground team was sent to Camp Schurman to attempt a climb of the Emmons glacier in hopes of reaching the stranded climbers. This team reported steady 50 mph winds with gusts to 75 mph at Camp Schurman (9,500 feet). Later that day, another team of rangers on helicopter standby was able to fly to Liberty Cap during a brief weather window. A "drop bag" containing emergency supplies was prepared for jettison to the climbers, but extreme winds prevented the helicopter from nearing them and the mission was aborted.

No communication was established with the climbers after June 17 and on June 18 the ground team reported a break in the weather. The helicopter was launched again and successfully inserted four rangers on the saddle between Liberty Cap and the true summit where they hiked to Catlett and Willcox and assisted them back to the landing zone for pickup. Catlett and Willcox were then flown to Madigan Army hospital where they were treated for severe dehydration and evaluated for possible renal complications.

Analysis
Catlett and Willcox became pinned down on the summit due to deteriorating weather. They felt that traveling on an unknown route over glaciers during whiteout conditions might endanger them more and they elected to dig in. Although there were brief periods of clear weather, it was felt that there was no substantial weather window to allow the party to break camp and safely get to a better location. This continued bad weather prevented movement and under recommendation from park personnel, the party stayed put.

It's common for Liberty Ridge climbing parties to carry-over the summit and descend an alternate route. This requires carrying heavy packs up the route and climbers are tempted to pack just enough food and fuel for the proposed length of their trip. Inclement weather can spell disaster for a party that is committed to the route. It is especially important for climbers ascending remote and harder routes on Rainier to carry additional food and fuel for possible storm-bound days.

This also applies to ascents on standard routes. It's worth noting that weather conditions worsened shortly after the rescue, and the mountain experienced extreme winds and cloudy weather for the next four days. (Source: Mike Gauthier, SAR Ranger, Mount Rainier National Park)

FALL ON SNOW, FAILURE TO SELF-ARREST
Washington, Columbia Peak
On July 13, Lee Giroux (50) and five other members of the Seattle Mountaineers attempted to reach the summit of Columbia Peak. The party left their camp at 6:00 a.m. that morning. Each party member was wearing a helmet and harness and carrying an ice ax. About 30 minutes into the climb there was about a 20 minute wait while Jim Tweedie, one of the trip leaders, scouted ahead to determine the route.

The party proceeded up to the toe of the glacier where Jim climbed a short rock gully, set up a belay and belayed Justin Merle and Lee up the pitch. Lee belayed the remaining party members up the pitch. Jim and Justin proceeded up the snow slope to a rock section thought to be the chimney section described in the route description. Upon reaching the rock section it was apparent that it did not match the route description. After reviewing the map and route description, it was decided that they would traverse up a 35 to 40 degree snow slope. The traverse was about 200 yards and was situated above a cliff band. Jim and Justin kicked steps up the slope to where it ended in rocks and heather and proceeded up to a high point. The rest of the party followed. They decided that they were not on the main summit of Columbia so Jim spent about 30 minutes scouting ahead to determine if it was feasible to get to the main summit from their position. After deciding that this was not feasible, the party decided to retrace their steps.

The day was warm, sunny and about 70 degrees F. The snow was soft and would accept an entire kicked boot. Crampons were not used because of the tendency to ball up in soft snow thereby not allowing the teeth to cut into the snow. The party retraced their steps on the traversing slope. Lee was the third person traversing the slope, and was followed by three other party members, including Jim. Lee had been traveling about 15 minutes and had just gone from holding his ax in his right hand to holding it in a two-handed self-belay hold and was traversing facing the slope. Lee's fall was not seen by the members of the climb; however, one party member did hear Lee hit the snow but could not distinguish the sound as either being a slip or a fall. This party member was closest and observed that Lee was falling on his back, head down with his ax somewhat underneath him on his right side. As Lee began to slide down the slope, all members observed that he did not make any attempt to self-arrest.

From the point he fell, Lee traveled about 75 feet down the snow slope along a ledge and over the cliff into a snow runnel. Jim and the other trip leader, Bob Hetzel, talked to the other members to determine if they felt comfortable in continuing down the slope. They were comfortable and proceeded down the slope slowly using ice axes for self-belay. Jim observed that the steps were not broken where Lee had fallen nor did he see marks indicating that Lee had attempted to self-arrest.

Bob was proceeding first and came to within 25 feet above Lee. He stepped into the snow runnel and began to move down. He made about three steps down when he heard someone yell, "Avalanche!" Bob dug his ax into the snow and put his head down. The snow flowed over Bob pushing him down about three to four feet. The avalanche carried Lee down approximately another 500 feet.

Bob stepped out of the snow runnel and proceeded down the slope as did the rest of the party. The snow ended in the rocks about 15 feet above Lee. Bob belayed Jim down to Lee while the rest of the party stayed on the rocks with Bob.

Jim found Lee in a face up position. Lee had sustained fatal trauma to the right temple area of his head. Jim determined the safest thing to do was to secure Lee in his existing location. Webbing was attached to Lee's harness and around a boulder. Jim climbed back up the 15 feet of rock to the other party members, and informed them that Lee was dead and that they would not attempt to move the body.

The group arrived back at Blanca Lake at 6:40 p.m. Jim hiked out to notify the Snohomish County Sheriff's Office. The next morning Jim flew back to Columbia Peak in the Search and Rescue helicopter and identified the location of Lee's body. Lee's helmet and ice ax were not found at the scene. The other party members left Blanca Lake and hiked out.

Analysis
Lee had ice ax arrest training, was an active climber, and had recently been on several climbs involving steep snow travel. Lee's training included how to self-arrest in this situation. However, traveling downhill on your back, head first, is the most difficult position from which to arrest. It is unknown why Lee did not attempt to self-arrest. (Source: From a report written by a panel of five members of the Seattle Mountaineers and written statements from party members)

FALLING ICE
Washington, Mount Rainier, Kautz Ice Cliff
On July 20 Mount Rainier communications received information relating to a 911 call from a climbing party on the Kautz Glacier route. The reporting climber Greg Prothman of Seattle Mountain Rescue called from Camp Hazard (11,300 feet) indicating that a party of three had been hit by falling ice from the Kautz Ice Cliff. One of the climbers, Tim Wentzer, had been seriously injured in the back and was in severe pain. Due to the location of the accident and severity of injuries, an Army Blackhawk was launched with a flight medic and flew directly to Camp Hazard. The medic was lowered to the accident scene and stabilized Wentzer in preparation for a winch raise into the Blackhawk. The Blackhawk flew Wentzer to Harborview trauma center in Seattle for treatment of a fractured C-7 vertebrae, other spinal complications and an injury to the knee.

Analysis
Wentzer's accident occurred in an area aptly called "The Chute" due to the amount of falling rock and ice. "The Chute" is the safest and fastest approach from Camp Hazard to the popular Kautz Glacier route. Rock and ice fall in "The Chute" is inevitable, therefore extreme caution and speed are advised when climbing or descending through this area. Wentzer was unfortunately in the wrong place at the wrong time. (Source: Mike Gauthier, SAR Ranger, Mount Rainier National Park)

FALL INTO CREVASSE
Washington, Mount Rainier, Emmons Glacier
On July 29, Don McIntyre and Joel Koury had just climbed Liberty Ridge and were forced to bivy near the summit of Rainier due to a sudden storm which deposited wet, heavy snow on the upper mountain. The team had lost the descent route in the weather and was making their way down the Emmons Glacier when Koury slipped while cleaning the wet snow from his crampons. Unable to arrest quickly in these conditions, Koury slid into McIntyre who was near the edge of the crevasse. Both fell and landed on a ledge system 25 to 30 feet below. McIntyre ruptured his aortic artery and Koury sustained knee, leg and hip injuries. McIntyre died a few hours later due to his injuries.

Ranger Kellogg was contacted by a climbing party of two descending the Emmons Glacier who reported that another team of two had taken a crevasse fall around 13,300 feet. One of the members was reported to be seriously injured, unconscious and having difficulty breathing. Kellogg relayed the information to White River ranger station and teams were assembled for a flight to assist with the rescue. Rangers Gauthier and Kellogg were climbing to the accident from Camp Schurman but were called back to join the other rescuers who were being shuttled to Emmons Flats where they awaited the arrival of a larger helicopter to insert the entire team close to the accident scene. At 7:30 p.m. a team of nine rangers was transported to the summit in an Army Chinook and ranger Brenchley led the hasty team of three to the accident scene to assess the situation while Gauthier organized the remaining rescuers for a technical lowering and possible crevasse extraction with litter. Upon arriving at the crevasse, Brenchley's team found Don McIntyre dead and his partner Joel Koury injured but ambulatory. At this point, the sun was setting and teams were restructured; Brenchley descended with Koury and six other rescuers back to Camp Schurman while Gauthier and Kellogg stayed at the crevasse with McIntyre to begin removal operations early the next morning.

The weather remained good the following day and plans were made to fly Koury and the seven rescuers out of the field while Gauthier and Kellogg prepared McIntyre's body for a hoist operation from 13,300 feet. Late morning mechanical problems prevented the Army helicopter from flight and a smaller helicopter was used to transport Koury and the team at Camp Schurman to Ranger Airfield. Unable to hoist with a small helicopter at such a high altitude, Gauthier's team secured the body well out of sight and away from the climbing route for an extraction when a suitable helicopter could be obtained. Weather and the heavy climbing activity prevented helicopter operations for the next five days. On Monday August 4, Rangers Gauthier, Yelverton and Olver were flown to the summit and down climbed to the hoist site. The Army Chinook was able to hoist the body and the team was picked up on the summit.

Analysis
The upper mountain of Rainier is notorious for sudden and unexpected storms that cover the climbing routes and leave climbers disoriented. The newly deposited wet snow made conditions very slick and was sticking to their crampons. Frequent "banging" with an ice ax was required to clean them and most climbers are unlikely to stop, anchor and then clean their crampons. Due to McIntyre's close proximity to the edge of the crevasse, there was little room for self arrest and a simple fall turned into a serious accident. (Source: Mike Gauthier, SAR Ranger, Mount Rainier National Park)

FALL INTO CREVASSE, GLISSADING INSTEAD OF WALKING, UNROPED
Washington, Mount Rainier, Inter Glacier
On August 3, Chris Kapaun was glissading unroped down the Inter Glacier and fell into a crevasse. His partner, Troy Hendrickson witnessed the fall and climbed back to Camp Schurman to report the accident. Rangers Puryear, Kellogg, M. Ronca and C. Ronca responded from the Camp Schurman ranger station with rescue litter and gear. Ranger M. Ronca descended into the crevasse and assessed Kapaun's injuries which included a compound fracture of the arm and possible head injuries. Kapaun had fallen 50 to 70 feet and was not wearing a helmet. With the assistance of other climbers, Kapaun was raised from the crevasse and packaged in a rescue litter. Rangers Gauthier and Olver climbed to the site and began the lowering to meet other ground teams which were assembling in Glacier Basin for a carry out. At the base on the Inter Glacier, Kapaun's injuries were reassessed, and it was determined that he could walk out on his own with the aid of rangers.

Analysis
The Inter Glacier is the primary route for climbers and skiers attempting Mount Rainier's Emmons Glacier. Although the glacier is small by comparison, it still has many large

crevasses and icy sections which necessitate one or two rescues every year. It is strongly recommended that climbers (especially those new to the area) rope up during all glacier travel, even on the Inter.

Glissading is a popular descent technique. However glacier conditions change weekly and old glissade paths frequently lead to newly exposed crevasses. Kapaun did not check his descent path and was unable to see what was ahead of him while sliding. Although the path may have been crevasse-free the week before, that was no longer the case. We strongly recommend that climbers hike down the Inter glacier, or at least check their descent path. (Source: Mike Gauthier, SAR Ranger, Mount Rainier National Park)

STRANDED—LOST, INADEQUATE CLOTHING AND EQUIPMENT
Washington, Mount Rainier, Disappointment Cleaver
Early on the morning of September 1, the two-person Connell party called Mount Rainier communications by cell phone to report that they had lost the climbing route in a white out and were unable to find their way up or down the mountain. Without any bivy gear, the party requested a rescue. Rangers Beilstein and Holien were notified at Camp Muir where they prepared for a climb and set out to locate the lost party. After three hours of climbing, the weather cleared and the rangers were able to make contact with them at 12,800 feet. They escorted the team back to their camp at 11,000 feet.

Analysis
The Connell party was climbing the popular Disappointment Cleaver route which normally has a well established boot track to the summit. It was reported to the party when they registered that storms during the preceding days had covered parts of the route. Carrying only fanny packs, the climbers did not have a map, compass or bivy gear and were unable to help themselves. Poor weather had been predicted and other parties reported seeing them head into the clouds earlier that morning. The route becomes entirely glaciated above 12,300 feet, and the climbers were unable to use any ground features for navigation.

Carrying the appropriate gear for a summit climb or day trip is strongly recommended, especially when foul weather is predicted and the route is difficult to follow. Although a cell phone enabled the climbers to request help, proper gear including map, compass and wands would have allowed them to find their route back to camp, thus avoiding the need for rescue. (Source: Mike Gauthier, SAR Ranger, Mount Rainier National Park)

FALL ON ICE, ICE SCREWS PULLED OUT—SOFT ICE, FATIGUE
Washington, Mount Rainier, Nisqually Glacier
Mount Rainier communications received a report of a fallen climber on the Nisqually Glacier from a cell phone call on September 6. The reporting party, a Seattle Mountaineers instructor, indicated that a climber in his group had fallen during ice climbing practice. The climber, Eric Brunson, was leading a moderate angle ice climb in a popular practice area on the Nisqually glacier. Brunson fell near the top of the climb shortly after placing his last ice screw. Due to soft ice conditions, all of his ice screws pulled out and Brunson fell to the ground, a distance greater than 40 feet. Brunson, who was wearing a helmet, sustained a possible back injury during the fall. His team members then moved him to a less hazardous area and the team called for a rescue.

A Jet Ranger helicopter met rangers Brenchley and Yelverton at the park helibase and inserted the team near the accident scene in a large serac field where they assessed Brunson's injuries and determined that he should be flown out immediately. Brunson, with a possible broken back, was prepared for flight while his group assisted rangers in preparing a better landing zone to prevent a difficult lowering. The pilot was required to pull power while on one and a half skids as Brunson was loaded into the ship. Brunson was flown to the helibase where he was transferred to an Airlift Northwest helicopter and flown to Harborview Medical Center in Seattle for treatment. His injuries included a compression fracture of T4 and T5 vertebrae and a fractured hip.

Analysis
Brunson's ice climbing experience was limited, and he may not have realized the dubious nature of protection in glacier ice under warm summer conditions. It's also worth noting that he reported feeling "gripped" at the top of his climb and was a little shaky when placing his last screw.

Ice protection is less than optimum even under "perfect" conditions. Scraping away surface slush and using long screws is strongly recommended when leading glacier ice under warm conditions. Confidence in one's abilities, especially in respect to placing gear on lead, is important.

It is also worth mentioning that the Mountaineers group was extremely prepared, having their own litter and descent route marked. Their assistance and preparedness helped to expedite this evacuation. (Source: Mike Gauthier, SAR Ranger, Mount Rainier National Park)

FALLING ROCKS, FALL ON ROCK, POOR POSITION
Washington, Lundin Peak
On September 10, Rob Crapo (37) successfully summitted Lundin Peak (6,057 feet) at 1330 with six members of the Seattle Mountaineers. Rob, an experienced climber with an extensive resume of climbs, was leading the trip. Peter Babler and Brendan Williams were rope leaders. The remaining four participants in the climb were students in the Basic Climbing Course.

On the descent, the party returned to the platform on the West Ridge where they had left their packs. Rob decided it was better for the party to rappel over a rock step there, rather than downclimb. Red webbing on a nearby tree indicated that other climbers had rappelled there. Rob set up a single rope rappel. Peter Babler and one of the Basic Students rappelled first, and as the third member started to rappel, Rob asked him to tell the other party members to move away from the bottom of the rappel.

While the others rappelled, Rob moved about 25 feet west on the platform, away from the rappel station. What happened next was somewhat unclear, as it appeared that he was either downclimbing or traversing to get a better look at the students on rappel. He was slightly below the platform when he remarked, "This is crap," referring to the quality of the rock. Moments later, at 1455, a large section of rock broke loose. Rob fell along with the rock. More rock and debris were torn loose in the ensuing rock slide, and Rob was tossed end over end among the tumbling boulders. He fell approximately 125 feet before coming to a stop. Peter and the student ran to get out of the path of the falling rock, but Peter was struck several times sustaining injuries to his right thigh, left arm, back, and right wrist.

Once the rock slide stopped, the climber on rappel was the first to reach Rob. Peter was incapacitated by his own injuries. Brendan quickly rappelled down and took control of the situation, noting that Rob was unconscious but with his helmet still on. He had sustained obvious, extensive injuries in the fall.

Two of the remaining party members went out for help. Meanwhile, Rob became more responsive. Brendan performed a more thorough examination of Rob's injuries, asking questions to which Rob responded. Rob asked what had happened and asked if his leg was broken. He also stated that the party should try to stick together.

Having witnessed the rockslide from neighboring Snoqualmie Mountain, father and son hikers Ron and Richard Riter descended toward the accident scene. After making voice contact with the Crapo party from the Snoqualmie-Lundin Saddle, Richard called 911 on his cellular phone to report the accident at 1510. He was transferred to King County Search and Rescue to confirm the accident site location. Richard and Ron descended the remaining distance to the accident site, and party member Neil Wachter used their phone to place another call to 911 and describe Rob's condition in detail. He was told that two MAST Black Hawk helicopters were being dispatched from Ft. Lewis. Other calls were made to seek medical advice.

In Redmond, Doug Caley of Seattle Mountain Rescue was paged at 1548 to respond to the accident. He drove to Snoqualmie Pass and hiked to the rescue scene with three other rescue personnel.

Rob's condition started to deteriorate quickly around 1630. His breathing became labored, shallow, irregular, and eventually stopped. Brendan started rescue breathing, but within a few minutes Rob's pulse had stopped. Two-person CPR was initiated with Brendan doing the rescue breathing and Neil the chest compressions. Rob did not respond to their efforts. Two helicopters arrived at the accident scene at 1815 and Rob was loaded into a basked for air evacuation. Although CPR was still being performed, Rob had become cold to the touch. Peter Babler was also evacuated by helicopter. The remaining party members hiked out after dark with the Caley rescue party, and were reunited with the two party members who had hiked out earlier. (Source: From report written by Seattle Mountaineers committee who reviewed the accident, and additional comments from the individuals involved)

Analysis
The section which Rob was downclimbing was not particularly challenging, and well within his abilities. This area is known for its poor rock quality. (Source: Barbara McCann, Climbing Committee Chair, Seattle Mountaineers)

(Editor's Note: I added the "poor position" to the title here. If the quality of the rock is known, then precautions such as positioning of participants and the guide is an important consideration.)

RAPPEL ANCHOR FAILURE, FALL ON ROCK
Washington, Mount Thompson, West Ridge
On September 17, two climbers had completed an ascent of Mount Thompson via the West Ridge and decided to rappel down the route instead of down-climbing the adjacent East Ridge (Class 3). The victim established the rappel line using a chockstone as an anchor. The partner stated that the anchor looked suspect and chose not to rappel

from it. The victim began a rappel and the chockstone failed. The victim fell about 200 feet, landing in a gully. The victim spent the night out while the partner went for help. The victim suffered fractures of the skull, vertebrae and pelvis, as well as acute hypothermia. (Source: Michael Mixon, Tacoma Mountain Rescue Unit)

(Editor's Note: Michael Mixon was not able to get ages, gender, and names of these climbers. Obviously the victim's partner chose the wiser course of letting the one who set the anchor go first. But there are some questions going begging here...

Some 1996 data came in, but is still incomplete. One report from May of 1996 involved eleven Seattle Mountaineers being avalanched on Red Mountain near Snoqualmie Pass. Nine of them were swept down a gully or over rock, falling as much as 100 feet. Nine were injured, two of them, including the leader, severely. The group had assessed the route for avalanche danger, but the soft snow travelled over the rock band they were on and caught them.

Of the several accidents included in the Washington data but not reported in the narratives, a few were in what can be called the "classic" category. These include crampons catching on pant legs while descending; at least five unbelayed novices, most on organized outings, unable to self-arrest; a stranded couple who simply needed to be re-directed to a walk-off route; a simple slip of less than two feet while descending a hand-line, resulting in a fractured ankle and an all-night rescue in the rain; two solo fatalities, one hiker and one climber, details unknown; and a "hand hold came off," resulting in a sixty foot fall. There were at least six other cases like the latter reported from other states this year.)

FALL ON ROCK, CLIMBING UNROPED, INADEQUATE EQUIPMENT—HIKING BOOTS—AND NO HARD HAT
West Virginia, River Rocks

On April 20, Mark Williamson (25) had finished a day of climbing and had already changed from his climbing shoes to his hiking boots. He reportedly spied a carabiner up a climb and decided to retrieve it. It was a 5.9+ route, but he did not change back to his rock shoes to rope up. About 20 feet he fell to rocky, sloping ground and rolled another 20 feet to land head down the slope, where the Rescue Squad found him. Squad call-out was at 6:30 p.m. and the Skills Team was called out at 6:45 p.m. when the need for a roped, belayed descent was determined.

Mark's initial vital signs were taken in the head-down position in which he was found. When he was transferred to a backboard and brought level, his vital signs began to drop significantly. In addition, extensive head abrasions and contusions were obvious, so helicopter transport was called. However, Mark's vital signs stabilized during the descent and remained stable thereafter. He was flown to UVA Hospital in Charlottesville, VA, and found to have a fractured vertebrate, abdominal injuries, and extensive abrasions with a few contusions. He recovered well and came back during the summer to thank his rescuers and apologize to the local landowner. (Source: Jim Underwood, Pendelton County Tactical Skills Team)

(Editor's Note: In situations like this, there must be a formula for calculating the ultimate price of a carabiner, etc., by determining the relationship between the climber's degree of desire and level of climbing skill.)

FALLS ON ROCK (4), CLIMBING UNROPED (3), FALLING ROCK— NO HELMET
Wisconsin, Devil's Lake State Park

There were five reports of climbing accidents from Devil's Lake this year, three of which resulted in fractures. The falling rock incident resulted in a concussion, as the victim was not wearing a helmet.

The average age of the victims was 22. Their skill levels and the difficulty of the routes were not included in the reports. There were an additional eleven "scrambling" incidents. These involve people getting off trail and slipping among loose rocks and boulders. All but one of the injuries in these cases were lacerations because of the nature of the rock. (Source: Steven Schmelzer, Park Ranger)

FALL ON SNOW—UNABLE TO SELF-ARREST, INEXPERIENCE, NO BELAY
Wyoming, Grand Teton National Park, Mount Teewinot

Chris Thompson (16) and Forrest Hill (?) had left Idaho Falls early the morning of June 6 to climb the East Face of Mount Teewinot. Thompson, being more experienced, was described as the leader, intent on providing instruction to Hill who had never before climbed on steep snow. Thompson was equipped with plastic boots, crampons, and a short Grivel ice tool. Hill was equipped with light Nike hiking shoes, crampons and a short Grivel ice tool borrowed from Thompson. Near 11,500 feet, Thompson and Hill put their crampons on. Within five minutes, the soft snow balled up under Thompson's crampons, causing him to slip. Thompson was unable to arrest his fall using his ice tool and slid down the snow slope picking up speed. Thompson estimates that he fell several hundred feet before falling into a "moat" (which he described as a horizontal crack in the snow separated by rock on the uphill side and snow on the downhill side). Thompson said that it took him over an hour to extricate himself, which likely explains why his partner was unable to locate him after the fall. Thompson then began his slow descent from the mountain.

Analysis

Based on information obtained in the interview, it seemed apparent that Hill was a beginning climber with essentially no experience, and Thompson was a novice climber with limited experience. Thompson was fortunate that he sustained only minor injuries. Without his early plunge into the opening, it is likely that Thompson's slide would have taken him over 1,000 feet down continuous steep snow and over multiple bands of steep rock. The arrival of Robert Keene, the mountaineer who assisted Hill to a safe location near tree line, initiated a search for Thompson, and then reported the incident to rangers, was a fortunate event which contributed to the overall positive outcome of this incident. (Source: Mark Magnuson, SAR Coordinator)

FALL ON ROCK—CAUSE UNKNOWN, CLIMBING ALONE
Wyoming, Grand Teton National Park, Grand Teton, Owen-Spaulding Route

On June 23 at 0825, Amer Beslagic (38) obtained a back-country camping permit at the Jenny Lake Ranger Station for a campsite at the Moraine in Garnet. His intention was to solo climb the Grand Teton via the Owen-Spaulding Route on the following day. From a high camp on the Moraine on June 24, he passed through the Lower Saddle and continued up a variation of the route via a couloir to the west. About 0830, a witness in the Lower Saddle observed Beslagic falling down the couloir from a location near the Upper Saddle. This witness and other climbers in the area traversed to Beslagic and confirmed that there were no signs of life. One of the climbers then descended to the valley to report the incident at the Jenny Lake Ranger Station. Grand Teton National Park rangers responded and recovered Beslagic's body from the mountain the same evening.

Analysis
It is difficult to assess Beslagic's experience as a climber, since he almost always climbed alone. The difficulty of his previous climbs do not seem to be of the same caliber as the Owen-Spaulding Route under the conditions of the route on June 24. Though Beslagic was on a steep and hazardous part of the climb, it was by no means the crux of the climb. The difficulties of the Owen-Spaulding Route were definitely ahead on the route. Witnesses stated that he appeared to be moving well and competently before the accident occurred.

The conditions on the upper part of the Owen-Spaulding Route at the time of the accident could best be described as extreme—similar to the conditions that would be encountered during a winter ascent. However, the portion of the climb where Beslagic fell was probably quite good at that particular time of day. The snow conditions at the place that Beslagic's body came to rest were described as frozen neve—perfect for crampons. The weather conditions at the time of the accident were clear and cold, but windy.

Beslagic appeared to have adequate equipment for climbing the section of the route on which he fell. He had mountain boots, crampons, ice ax and appropriate clothing. He did not take a rope, which would have been very useful higher on the climb. Since he did not have a partner, it is unlikely that he would have used a rope to belay himself on the couloir where he fell. Beslagic did not have a climbing helmet that was found at the scene nor was a helmet seen by witnesses. A helmet would not have been a factor in surviving a fall of this magnitude.

It is unclear exactly why Beslagic fell. He apparently lost his ice ax at the beginning of his slide. As the investigating ranger on scene stated that under the conditions in the Idaho Express on the day of the accident, a self-arrest would have had to be performed immediately to be of any use. Possibilities for the cause of the accident include Beslagic being blown over by a gust of wind or just losing his balance and dropping his ice tool.

Beslagic was well informed about the route, its current difficult conditions, and the hazards of soloing. He received this information from a park ranger when he obtained his back-country permit, other climbers on the mountain and in the valley, and from informational brochures and trailhead signs. He apparently had a sufficient command of the English language to understand these warnings. (Source: Rich Perch, SAR Ranger)

FALL ON SNOW, UNABLE TO SELF-ARREST, ILLNESS
Wyoming, Grand Teton National Park, Grand Teton
On June 25 at 1300, Exum Guide Jim Kanzler reported to park dispatch via cellular phone an accident in Garnet Canyon. According to Kanlzer, Paul Newman (38) had sustained injuries in a 500 foot fall down snow at the Lower Saddle headwall. Newman's partner, Moir Bowman (38), was able to assist him down to the Garnet Meadows where he reportedly collapsed in pain. Newman's chief complaint was severe pain the lower

back and hip, with a "grating sensation" on movement.

Rescue coordinator Mark Magnuson requested the park contract helicopter, which arrived at Lupine Meadows at 1330. Ranger Eric Gabriel responded to the scene from the Lower Saddle, arriving about 1335. Ranger Bill Culbreath responded from the summit of Disappointment Peak, arriving at 1345. After obtaining patient information from Gabriel and consultation with medical control, Lanny Johnson, rangers Leo Larson and George Montopoli were flown to the Garnet Meadows with medical equipment. Newman was immobilized in a full body vacuum splint, placed on a backboard, and carried a short distance to the helicopter. He was flown from the scene to St. John's Hospital, arriving at 1455. Newman was treated for severe, deep contusions to his lower back and hip.

Analysis
According to Newman's climbing partner, the two had ascended to the Lower Saddle from their campsite on the Moraine early that morning. As Newman was not feeling well, they decided to return to camp. At the top of the Lower Saddle headwall, which was covered with steep, hard snow, Newman removed his crampons and initiated a glissade. Losing control and unable to self-arrest, he slid approximately 500 feet down the headwall, "tumbling" several times near the bottom until he came to rest at the runout of the slope. Newman was able to stand and, with assistance, self-evacuate down to the Garnet Meadows where he was unable to continue due to the pain. (Source: Mark Magnuson, SAR Coordinator)

FALL ON ROCK, INADEQUATE BELAY and PROTECTION
Wyoming, Grand Teton National Park, Grand Teton, Owen-Spaulding
On July 4 at 0925, Jackson Hole Mountain Guide Allan Bard (44) took a fatal leader fall while guiding on the Owen- Spaulding Route on the Grand Teton. He and his client, Jay Wiener, were on a section of the route known as the Double Chimney when the accident occurred. Bard fell approximately 130 feet to the end of the rope before his fall was arrested. Other climbers in the area became aware of the accident and came to Wiener's assistance, but they were unable to reach Bard. Grand Teton National Park climbing rangers learned about the accident and dispatched the Bridger-Teton contract helicopter and rescue team. A rescue team member rappelled to Bard at 1533 and confirmed that he was dead. Rangers traversed with Bard's body to the Upper Saddle. Plans to evacuate the body with the helicopter were abandoned when a storm moved through the area. The rescue team spent the night at the hut at the Lower Saddle and returned to Bard's location early on the morning of July 6. At 1008 they were able to use the contract helicopter to fly Bard to a heli-spot in Lupine Meadows where his body was turned over to Teton County Coroner Bob Campbell.

Analysis
A properly executed belay and placement of intermediate protection most likely would have made the difference between this being a fatality or a shorter fall resulting in only minor injuries to Allan Bard. According to guide Andy Carson and other guides in the area, it is not uncommon for guides to forego a belay on ground where a fall is deemed to be unlikely. The reason for this is both to enhance the speed of the ascent and because of a concern that an inexperienced client might pull the guide off the climb. In the mountain setting where weather is unpredictable and daylight is a precious commodity,

the speed of the ascent often equates to safety in the minds of mountain guides and some climbers. The time it takes to set up a belay can slow their ascent. Clients are often inexperienced at the art of belaying, and some guides prefer to climb without a belay and instruct the client not to touch the rope. This, of course, leaves no room for error on the part of the guide.

The equipment used by Bard and his client performed exceptionally well and probably had no bearing on the cause of this accident. The rope and harness took an extreme fall and was apparently undamaged. It was fortunate that a single stopper placed at the belay held or the fall would certainly have resulted in a second fatality. Both guide and client were properly clothed, and were equipped with climbing helmets, crampons, and ice axes.

It is not clear exactly why Bard fell from the Double Chimney. The conditions at the time of the accident were very poor, with snow and verglas, though the route was certainly within the abilities of Bard. The other climbers in the area did not observe any rock or ice falling from above that would have caused the accident. They did, however, describe rock and ice falling concurrently with Bard. It is possible that he pulled off a loose hold or that the debris that was observed was caused by his fall in the chimney.

There was an extended period of time between the accident and the first rescuer reaching Bard's body. Teton County Coroner Bob Campbell stated that only the immediate placement of a tourniquet could have made any difference in the end. It is unlikely that someone could have rappelled to Bard following the accident and properly treated his injuries fast enough to save his life.

Bard was climbing well within his abilities. He was well known and respected by other climbers for both his climbing ability and guiding. He apparently had an accident-free record throughout his career as a climber and guide. He was also reported to be very fit and well rested at the time of the accident. (Source: Rich Perch, SAR Ranger)

RAPPEL ERROR—INADEQUATE PROTECTION, FALL ON ROCK, INEXPERIENCE IN OUTDOOR CLIMBING, WEATHER
Wyoming, Grand Teton National Park, Symmetry Spire

On July 7, around 1600, John Hehr (48) fell to his death when his rappel anchor on the Southwest Ridge route of Symmetry Spire failed. The rappel anchor failed while the climbing party (J. Hehr specifically) was descending the Southwest Ridge route after experiencing a significant storm about one rope length (50m) from the top of the route. He was accompanied on the route by two other climbers: his stepson, Demian Farnworth, and a friend, Kevin Kerwin. Angie Stika, the stepson's girlfriend, had accompanied them on the approach earlier that morning, but had turned around about 0730 because she was not feeling well. Two other climbers in the area, Mike Lanza and Gerald Prutsman, were the first to make contact with Hehr. (Farnworth and Kerwin were still descending.) After verifying that Hehr was dead and that Farnworth and Kerwin were all right, they departed the scene to report the accident. They encountered Ranger Julena Campbell on the Jenny Lake trail, reported the accident to her, and she radioed the initial report to Grand Teton National Park dispatch immediately. Grand Teton National Park climbing rangers were mobilized about 1900, and the Bridger-Teton contract helicopter was summoned. Rangers Jim Phillips and Ron Johnson were flown to the scene to confirm the fatality and check on the status of the other two climbing party members. Rangers Bill Alexander and Scott Guenther were dispatched to accompany and assist the descending party members. After consulting with Lanny Johnson, Medical Advisor, and verifying that Farnworth and Kerwin were still experiencing no problems on the descent, the decision was made to evacuate the body on the following day due to the approaching darkness.

Analysis
Hehr fastened himself into the rappel system and just prior to weighting the system said, "I hope this flake holds."

This incident is an example of a situation where technical climbing ability greatly exceeds experience in an actual mountain environment. Farnworth was a 5.11 climber in a gym and had no problem with the level of climbing on the Southwest Ridge (5.6 or 5.7). Yet he had difficulty in protecting the route, and he did not back up his rappel anchor with artificial protection because he "did not trust protection that he placed." In a subsequent rappel, his partner noticed another anchor failure that occurred as Farnworth was just finishing his rappel. Sport climbers who turn to the mountains for additional adventure should note that altitude, weather, placement of protection, and so forth are all part of the activity.

When situations become complicated by intense weather, experience plays a major role in the decision-making process. After some discussion, the party made the reasonable decision to retreat by rappelling the route. Earlier they did have the opportunity to join up with another group above them, who were trailing a rope that had become stuck (for the second time). They simply "unstuck" the rope for them and never requested any assistance, such as a belay up the final pitch. In addition, once they had decided to retreat, perhaps a more reasonable approach would have been for Kerwin, who had more mountain experience and had climbed the route before, to play a more active role in setting up the rappel stations.

The group was making extremely slow progress on the approach. They were forced to circumnavigate the snow which they were not equipped to travel on. Most likely they did not begin climbing the route until after 1100. They should have been aware of the unstable weather since they had been stormed-off Guide's Wall the previous day, and of the strong afternoon thundershowers which had been forecast. They continued to climb even when the storm's arrival was imminent.

Early starts, proper attire, knowledge of weather, and solid decision making play a major role in preventing hypothermia, and this may have played a major role in the team's actions. They were forced to huddle and wait for breaks in an intense storm in a very exposed location subject to high winds along with the precipitation. Their attire in general was questionable as well. There was substantial confusion between Farnworth and Kerwin in setting up the rappel that failed for Hehr.

Although it mostly likely would not have made a difference in Hehr's demise, only Kerwin was wearing a helmet. The fact that Farnworth and Hehr were not using helmets reflects once again on their inexperience in the actual mountain environment. (Source: George Montopoli, Park Ranger)

FALL ON ROCK—CHANGE OF PLANS
Wyoming, Devil's Tower National Monument
On August 21 at 1450, the Visitor Center received a report from Lucas Bannister that a climber was calling for help on the Southwest Buttress. I notified Ranger Fontaine to organize the SAR team for a possible rescue and then responded to the Tower Trail with

rangers Martin and Drane-Martin. We located the individual, and Drane-Martin, an EMT, and I climbed to his location on the Southwest Buttress. When we arrived we contacted Kenneth Pisichko (49) and two friends, Craig Spakowski and Ray Kenny. Pisichko said that they had registered to climb the Durrance Route (5.6), but there were other climbers on it, so they decided to do the first pitch of Direct Southwest (5.7). Pisichko slipped and fell about six feet, catching and breaking his right ankle on a ledge. Sam Shafer, a local climber and nurse/ paramedic, had already contacted Pisichko and splinted his right leg. Pisichko was alert, oriented x 3, and relatively comfortable. He had already taken four Tylenol 4's that he had with him. He had pulse distal to the fracture. He advised us that he was diabetic and that he had taken insulin earlier in the day. His vitals at 1545 were P/74, R/12. Four other climbers, Jim Bernard, Matt Lisenby, Jason Cushner, and Lynn Lee, were on the Tower and volunteered to assist with the rescue.

At 1615 the SAR team reached the top of the boulder field below the Southwest Buttress. Using one of the climber's ropes, we hauled up a 300 foot static line. That was anchored and used to bring up ranger Gallant with the litter. Pisichko was secured in the litter, his vitals were taken (P/102, R/20) and, accompanied by ranger Gallant, was lowered about 160 feet to the boulder field. The lower was completed at 1721. (Source: Jim Schlinkmann, Chief Ranger)

Analysis
Here was a climber mentally prepared to do one route of a certain level of difficulty who then changed his route choice due to circumstances described. Being faced with a new objective and a degree of difficulty higher than anticipated has often contributed to the actual cause—in this case a fall—of an accident. (Source: Jed Williamson)

(Editor's Note: This was the only climbing accident recorded at Devil's Tower this year.)

FALL ON ROCK, FALL INTO MOAT, CLIMBING ALONE
Wyoming, Grand Teton, Mount Teewinot
On August 22, Larry L. Fahlberg (44) died while attempting a solo climb of the East Face Route on Mount Teewinot in Grand Teton National Park. Fahlberg was climbing alone and the accident was not witnessed. He was reported overdue from the climb by a friend on the following day, and a search was implemented the same afternoon. A total of 48 people were involved in search efforts from Grand Teton and Yellowstone National Parks, USFS helitack crew and pilot, Teton County Search and Rescue and Exum Mountain Guides. Field search teams were comprised of technical climbers, search dog teams and aerial reconnaissance.

Fahlberg's body was located by Grand Teton National Park rangers on August 24 in a moat at the 11,000 foot level on the East Face route. He had apparently fallen approximately 30 feet and died of his injuries and hypothermia. Fahlberg was raised from the moat and his body was flown by helicopter to Lupine Meadows and turned over to the Teton County Coroner at 1400.

Analysis
By all accounts Fahlberg was an experienced climber and very familiar with the Teton Range. The route he was attempting was well within his abilities. The conditions found on the route the day of the accident were relatively good and a solo ascent by a climber with Fahlberg's experience was not unusual or unreasonable. He was appropriately

equipped for the climb in the conditions found on August 22. No ice ax was found at the scene, but it is likely that Fahlberg had one with him that was not found. An ax would not have been of benefit if Fahlberg was on rock or stepping from snow to rock when the accident occurred. He was apparently not wearing crampons during the accident, but these would have been a hindrance on the terrain he was climbing.

Fahlberg was an experienced climber and would have been well aware of the dangers of solo climbing. Lack of a climbing partner/witness as well as the uncertainty of his climbing plans were a factor in the search for Fahlberg. These factors, however, would have no effect on the outcome of this case according to Teton County Coroner Bob Campbell. It is highly unlikely that Fahlberg could have survived his injuries even in the time it would have taken to effect the swiftest of rescues. (Climbing registration is no longer required at Grand Teton National Park, but a voluntary sign-out service is available for those who still prefer to have their whereabouts monitored.)

From the interviews and evidence found, the following is a likely scenario. Fahlberg would have followed through with his intent to drive from Cooke City early on the morning of August 27, and left early from Lupine Meadows parking area. The morning was warm and he would have stripped off his jacket and hat and worn his visor and sunglasses. He was very fit and would have moved rapidly. Rick Kneedler most likely watched Fahlberg ascend the snowfield through his binoculars immediately before his accident at 1020. The old set of boot tracks ascended the snowfield directly to its highest point where there was a gap between the snow and the rock that had melted out. A newer set of tracks off to the side provided a more secure route, but was not evident from below. Possibilities for the cause of Fahlberg's fall into the moat are a slip on the rock with wet/snowy boots, a portion of the snow breaking away as he stepped across the gap, or rockfall striking Fahlberg while he was in an exposed position. He probably fell the 30 feet into the moat and possibly lost consciousness momentarily. Upon awakening he would have placed his extra clothes and hat on as well as his rain jacket since he would have been in the spray of ice water. It was dark in the moat and he would have placed his headlamp on his head and turned it on. All this was in preparation for a climb out of the moat. However, Fahlberg had sustained a major head injury as well as being hypothermic, and he lost consciousness before being able to extract himself. Fahlberg may have untied his own shoe laces prior to his death. (It is not unusual for hypothermia victims to undress themselves in the later stages of that condition.) The food in his pack was apparently untouched, which supports the idea that the accident occurred on the ascent as opposed to the descent. (Source: Rich Perch, SAR Ranger)

(Editor's Note: This was the third incident on Mount Teewinot for the summer. The one not reported in these narratives was also a fall on snow—but on the descent. The victim fell 200 feet into a six-foot deep moat. In all these cases, there was no belay or self-arrest. This year's fatality and serious injury numbers are certainly high for this category.)

FALL ON ROCK, PROTECTION PULLED OUT
Wyoming, Grand Teton National Park, Grand Teton

On August 22 at 1143, Ranger Leo Larson was at the Lower Saddle when he received word of a possible incident on the Lower Exum Ridge of the Grand Teton. Additional information received from Exum Guide Mark Newcomb via cellular phone indicated that a climber had taken a significant fall on the Lower Exum and that cries for help were coming from the scene. Larson prepared to respond to the scene with park employee Jack McConnell and emergency hire Steve Griffin.

Based on available information, Ranger Mark Magnuson, Rescue Coordinator for the day, requested the contract helicopter respond to Lupine Meadows. Exum Guides Doug Chabot and Wes Bunch, who were above the Lower Saddle, received word of the accident and proceeded directly to the scene.

Chabot and Bunch climbed the first three pitches of the Lower Exum and arrived on scene at 1235. They reported a 32 year old male who had taken a 40 to 50 foot leader fall, sustaining superficial lacerations to the head, hands, and arms, and banged up knees. The victim was alert and oriented, had not lost consciousness, and was ambulatory. The party's intent after the accident had been to rappel the route, but their rope was shredded in the fall, Ranger Larson and his team, who traversed onto the Lower Exum via Wall Street Couloir, arrived on scene at 1250 and performed additional patient assessment. Following consultation with Dr. Rick McKay at St. John's Hospital emergency room, the decision was made to assist the injured climber, Don Saver, down to the Lower Saddle. Full consideration was given to a thorough neurological examination prior to this decision, which was agreed to by the patient.

Larson and party assisted Saver down to the Lower Saddle by traversing back across the Wall Street Couloir, then down the Owen Couloir. Upon arrival at the Saddle, Saver was flown by helicopter to Lupine Meadows, with ranger Jim Phillips attending. He was then transported by ground ambulance to St. John's Hospital where he was treated for multiple lacerations and contusions.

Analysis

In a follow-up interview with Saver, he stated that he was leading what appeared to be the third pitch of the Lower Exum route when he lost his grip on the smooth slab and fell. He pulled three pieces of protection during the fall: a small three cam unit, a fixed pin, then a #1 Metolious 4 cam unit. The rope snagged over a rock horn, stopping Saver's fall about 15 feet above a ledge. An examination of the rope (10.5 mm Blue Water) at the point where it snagged the horn, revealed approximately 36 to 48 inches of exposed core (sheath gone), with three internal strands broken. An examination of what is believed to be the 4 cam unit revealed deep scratches/gouges to the curved cam faces. No examination of the other two pieces was possible.

Saver is likely quite fortunate the rope snagged the horn described and performed as it was intended. He was also wearing a helmet, which likely contributed to the minor nature of his injuries. Saver described his fall as "pure air, bouncing several times against the rock." (Source: Mark Magnuson, SAR Coordinator)

(Editor's Note: The victim is also fortunate that rangers and guides were able to respond expeditiously to the scene.)

LOSS OF CONTROL—VOLUNTARY GLISSADE, CLIMBING ALONE, NO HARD HAT
Wyoming, Wind River Canyon, Dinwoody Pass

On September 1, Steve Fleming (45) was unable to self-arrest while descending from Dinwoody Pass. In a report he submitted, he stated that the snowfield he ascended in the morning required crampons, but had softened in the afternoon to the point where "my ice ax would not hold as my brake." He said he slid over 100 yards, striking many exposed rocks. He as able to slow his descent somewhat by rolling onto his back and digging in his heels.

Analysis
This accident could have been avoided if I had taken the time to test conditions. It would also have helped if I had used the shaft end of my ax, not the point.

Because of a severely sprained ankle and a gash on the back of my head, I was medivacked to the hospital in Jackson. I also received excellent help from other climbers in the area.... (Source: Steve Fleming)

FALL ON ROCK, RAPPEL ROPES KNOT "UNRAVELED"
Wyoming, Grand Teton, Guide's Wall
On September 13, Karen Turk (32) Matt Goewert (33), and Carrie Dagher were descending Guide's Wall when this incident occurred. Goewert and Dagher stated that the party of three had climbed the Guide's Wall route to within two pitches of the top. At this point, Turk elected to remain while Goewert and Dagher finished the route. In preparation for their descent, Goewert tied both their ropes together using an overhand knot, leaving about six to eight inches of tail. One rope was 10mm in diameter and described as new, the other rope a 10.5mm in diameter was described as used. Goewert and Dagher each rappelled down to Turk's position, then the three of them each rappelled once down to the next station. At this point, Goewert started to untie the knot by loosening it (for a single rope rappel) then decided to keep the ropes tied together as the final rappel would be another long, double rope rappel. Goewert re-secured the knot by pulling on all ends to tighten, which he demonstrated. The ropes were threaded through three rappel rings which were secured by multiple pieces of webbing tied around a tree. Goewert then rappelled approximately 80 to 90 feet to the next ledge. When Goewert finished this rappel, Dagher said that she and Turk moved the knot about twelve inches forward, but did not adjust it. Turk then proceeded to rappel. When Turk was approximately 30 feet above the ledge, Dagher states that she watched the knot "unravel," causing Turk to fall. Turk fell about 15 to 20 feet, struck her back against a rock prow, then fell another ten to 15 feet onto the ledge, landing on her back.

Goewert said that Turk never lost consciousness, but was in significant pain. In conducting a physical assessment of Turk, he found a large laceration across her lower back, with exposed spine, but no other significant injuries. His treatment included care and comforting of the patient and monitoring vital signs. Dagher reported the incident via Goewert's cell phone.

Analysis
Goewert, an experienced lead climber, said that he's been using the overhand knot for a couple of years, but has always been a little uncomfortable with it. He added that it's a knot used by a lot of climbers he knows. He's not sure why the knot came untied. It had held multiple rappels and, after having been loosened, had been re-secured by himself and rappelled on once again. Goewert added that he would no longer use this knot.

In a phone interview with Turk on the morning of September 13, she described herself as fairly new to climbing, having started in May of this year. She said she has climbed a lot in Illinois, but this was her first "alpine" route. She could offer no additional information surrounding the nature of the accident, but added that Dagher had made a comment about the knot, to the effect that "it looked pretty weird" and she wasn't clear how it could hold. This comment was made at the last rappel station. Turk said she was aware that Goewert had adjusted the knot at this station but did not see him do so.

Turk described her injuries as tissue only, with no fractures. The wound (approximately four inches long and one inch wide) had been surgically cleaned and sutured, but she was unsure as to the number of sutures required. (Source: Mark Magnuson, SAR Coordinator)

(Editor's Note: This method of tying the ends of two climbing ropes together started to appear recently, being referred to as a "Euro-guide knot." One theory behind the use of the knot is that it does not snag as easily as other choices. Another theory is that it is easier to untie than a double fisherman's or figure of eight after the strain of several rappellers. This later theory certainly appears to be true!)

FALL ON ROCK, CLIMBING ALONE, INADEQUATE CLOTHING AND EQUIPMENT, INEXPERIENCE
Wyoming, Grand Teton National Park, Disappointment Peak

On October 5 at 1245, John Jay Leach (23) fell to his death while climbing up cliffs above Amphitheater Lake. He fell an estimated 150 feet from or near the East Chimney route on Disappointment Peak at an elevation of approximately 10,000 feet. Leach had been on a day hike to the lake with six companions where he separated from them with the intention of climbing the mountain. Unassociated hikers in the area witnessed the accident and went to his assistance, but determined that he had died in the fall. Mitchell Smith had also witnessed the fall and hiked down to a phone at Jenny Lake Ranger Station to report the incident to Grand Teton National Park officials. Two park rangers were flown to a heli-spot at Amphitheater Lake and then climbed to the victim, confirming that he died of head injuries. Leach was flown by helicopter sling load to the Lupine Meadows Rescue Cache where his body was turned over to the Teton County Coroner.

Analysis

John Jay Leach was a novice climber with minimal formal training who was on very technical terrain. The investigation revealed that his experience was limited to some rappelling but no roped climbing. The cliffs that he fell from are moderate fifth class terrain where the great majority of experienced climbers would feel the need to be roped. Loose rock is always a consideration in the Teton range and could have been a factor in this incident.

He was not properly equipped to do an ascent of Disappointment Peak by the route he had chosen. He had no rope, harness, climbing protection or partner with him. Additionally he was dressed only in shorts, t-shirts and running shoes. Leach was not wearing a climbing helmet, although this piece of equipment would not have mitigated the injuries incurred in the severe fall and was not a factor.

This was apparently his first trip to Amphitheater Lake and he was unfamiliar with the Teton range. Leach would have passed a sign at the Lupine Meadows trailhead warning that mountain climbing is a hazardous activity and that loose rock was common in the range. This also advised that proper equipment and training were necessary. At least one of his companions had tried to convince him to stay with the group, but Leach seemed determined to ignore this advice and strike out on his own. He was an accomplished Nordic skier, and was reportedly extremely fit. The climb of Disappointment Peak as well as the choice of the route seemed to be based upon impulse. (Source: Rich Perch, SAR Ranger)

(Editor's Note: This was the fifth fatality in the Grand Teton range this year. In this example, the victim was a hiker-turned-climber, and so must be reported as such. It is the kind of case that often results in climbing being characterized as a "marginal" activity.

One final report from the Grand Tetons involved this editor. I was guiding on the Owen-Spaulding. A climber in the party ahead of me dislodged a softball-sized rock that fell about 50 feet and hit me on top of the head. The result was a laceration and a lump, because unfortunately, I had lent my helmet to a client who didn't have one. I was able to continue the climb. Lucky. The lessons are clear.)

TABLE I
REPORTED MOUNTAINEERING ACCIDENTS

	Number of Accidents Reported		Total Persons Involved		Injured		Fatalities	
	USA	CAN	USA	CAN	USA	CAN	USA	CAN
1951	15		22		11		3	
1952	31		35		17		13	
1953	24		27		12		12	
1954	31		41		31		8	
1955	34		39		28		6	
1956	46		72		54		13	
1957	45		53		28		18	
1958	32		39		23		11	
1959	42	2	56	2	31	0	19	2
1960	47	4	64	12	37	8	19	4
1961	49	9	61	14	45	10	14	4
1962	71	1	90	1	64	0	19	1
1963	68	11	79	12	47	10	19	2
1964	53	11	65	16	44	10	14	3
1965	72	0	90	0	59	0	21	0
1966	67	7	80	9	52	6	16	3
1967	74	10	110	14	63	7	33	5
1968	70	13	87	19	43	12	27	5
1969	94	11	125	17	66	9	29	2
1970	129	11	174	11	88	5	15	5
1971	110	17	138	29	76	11	31	7
1972	141	29	184	42	98	17	49	13
1973	108	6	131	6	85	4	36	2
1974	96	7	177	50	75	1	26	5
1975	78	7	158	22	66	8	19	2
1976	137	16	303	31	210	9	53	6
1977	121	30	277	49	106	21	32	11
1978	118	17	221	19	85	6	42	10
1979	100	36	137	54	83	17	40	19
1980	191	29	295	85	124	26	33	8
1981	97	43	223	119	80	39	39	6
1982	140	48	305	126	120	43	24	14
1983	187	29	442	76	169	26	37	7
1984	182	26	459	63	174	15	26	6
1985	195	27	403	62	190	22	17	3
1986	203	31	406	80	182	25	37	14
1987	192	25	377	79	140	23	32	9
1988	156	18	288	44	155	18	24	4
1989	141	18	272	36	124	11	17	9
1990	136	25	245	50	125	24	24	4
1991	169	20	302	66	147	11	18	6
1992	175	17	351	45	144	11	43	6

	Number of Accidents Reported		Total Persons Involved		Injured		Fatalities	
	USA	CAN	USA	CAN	USA	CAN	USA	CAN
1993	132	27	274	50	121	17	21	14
1994	158	25	335	58	131	25	27	5
1995	168	24	353	50	134	18	37	7
1996	139	28	261	59	100		31	6
1977	149	35	308	87	142	24	28	13
Totals	4805	702	8686	1479	4096	559	1155	248

TABLE II

	1951–1996			1997		
Geographical Districts	Number of Accidents	Deaths	Total Persons Involved	Number of Accidents	Deaths	Total Persons Involved
Canada						
Alberta	358	104	775	25	8	67
British Columbia	253	100	553	7	3	26
Yukon Territory	33	26	73	0	0	0
Ontario	33	8	61	0	0	0
Quebec	27	7	58	2	1	4
East Arctic	7	2	20	1	0	1
West Arctic	1	1	2	0	0	0
Practice Cliffs[1]	13	2	18	0	0	0
United States						
Alaska	375	150	560	10	4	36
Arizona, Nevada Texas	57	11	111	7	0	10
Atlantic–North	685	100	1158	25	0	45
Atlantic–South	65	15	104	2	5	1
California	943	233	1972	27	2	51
Central[2]	112	11	185	8	2	8
Colorado/Oklahoma	592	177	1015	13	2	25
Montana, Idaho South Dakota	62	23	95	1	2	2
Oregon	132	62	319	8	2	14
Utah, New Mexico	110	37	198	3	2	4
Washington	895	266	1597	31	5	60
Wyoming	452	100	827	24	6	48

[1]This category includes bouldering, as well as artificial climbing walls, buildings, and so forth. These are also added to the count of each state and province, but not to the total count, though that error has been made in previous years.

[2]The two fatalities occurred in Minnesota at Taylor's Falls, located in Interstate Park.

(Editor's Note: The Practice Cliffs category has been removed from the U.S. data.)

TABLE III

	1951–96 USA	1959–96 CAN.	1997 USA	1997 CAN.
Terrain				
Rock	3464	415	100	12
Snow	2038	303	43	9
Ice	182	87	7	13
River	13	3	0	0
Unknown	22	6	0	1
Ascent or Descent				
Ascent	3060	439	100	19
Descent	1891	295	47	15
Unknown[3]	247	3	2	1
Immediate Cause				
Fall or slip on rock	2392	222	72	9
Slip on snow or ice	774	154	33	11
Falling rock, ice or object	479	106	16	4
Exceeding abilities	399	27	19	0
Avalanche	253	106	3	1
Exposure	234	12	3	1
Illness[1]	269	20	10	1
Stranded	258	5	9	3
Rappel Failure/Error	196	35	12	3
Loss of control/glissade	166	15	2	1
Fall into crevasse/moat	129	41	3	0
Failure to follow route	121	25	5	2
Nut/chock pulled out	97	3	3	0
Piton pulled out	84	12	0	0
Faulty use of crampons	65	5	4	0
Lightning	39	6	0	1
Skiing	48	9	0	0
Ascending too fast	43	0	0	0
Equipment failure	7	2	0	0
Other[2]	181	23	21	1
Unknown	59	8	0	0
Contributory Causes				
Climbing unroped	889	146	13	4
Exceeding abilities	828	167	8	8
Inadequate equipment/clothing	541	70	11	1
Placed no/inadequate protection	463	64	30	11
Weather	369	50	9	7
Climbing alone	316	54	9	3
No hard hat	227	23	16	1
Nut/chock pulled out	169	16	12	0
Darkness	114	18	4	1
Party separated	97	16	3	1
Piton pulled out	82	10	2	0

	1951–96 USA	1959–96 CAN.	1997 USA	1997 CAN.
Contributory Causes (cont.)				
Poor position	107	13	4	2
Inadequate belay	107	18	7	2
Failure to test holds	66	18	1	0
Exposure	55	11	1	2
Failed to follow directions	60	5	4	0
Illness[1]	32	4	0	0
Equipment failure	9	4	0	2
Other[2]	227	79	7	0
Age of Individuals				
Under 15	112	11	0	1
15-20	1142	196	19	1
21-25	1422	222	30	3
26-30	1023	187	28	2
31-35	669	95	15	1
36-50	824	105	24	3
Over 50	128	18	4	2
Unknown	888	466	52	111
Experience Level				
None/Little	1471	280	31	0
Moderate (1 to 3 years)	1332	340	29	0
Experienced	1336	359	50	0
Unknown	1437	264	62	124
Month of Year				
January	178	14	9	1
February	177	37	2	3
March	238	46	5	2
April	328	29	10	0
May	705	47	17	1
June	830	54	24	3
July	911	215	30	5
August	840	124	28	13
September	1048	48	11	1
October	335	29	9	1
November	152	5	3	5
December	61	17	1	0
Unknown	4	0	0	0
Type of Injury/Illness (Data since 1984)				
Fracture	691	132	68	14
Laceration	364	51	45	6
Abrasion	203	39	18	0
Bruise	224	57	33	2
Sprain/strain	178	20	11	1
Concussion	115	13	18	1
Frostbite	77	7	9	1
Hypothermia	97	11	8	1

	1951–96 USA	1959–96 CAN.	1997 USA	1997 CAN.
Type of Injury/Illness (cont.)				
Dislocation	67	6	4	2
Puncture	27	4	0	1
Acute Mountain Sickness	17	0	4	1
HAPE	49	0	0	0
HACE	16	0	0	0
Other[3]	183	31	10	0
None	103	68	22	0

[1]These included: diabetes (1), AMS (4), HACE (1), hypothermia (2), fatigue (6), frostbite (7), shoulder dislocation (1).

[2]These included: unable to self-arrest (16), failure to turn back (2), route selected had extreme objective dangers (1), late start, carabiner broke, inattention (3), handhold came off (3), rock roof collapsed—unfamiliar with type of rock, wind gust knocked climber off summit, jumped crevasse—landed on ice, unable to free snow from crampons (2), miscommunication (2), inadequate food, homemade rivet hanger failed, jumars "failed"—came off rope.

Rappel errors included: rope ends uneven (2), rope entangled, ropes too short, forgot to untie safety knot in end of rappel rope—knot jammed in anchor ring.

[3]These included: pneumothorax (5), severe dehydration (3), punctured lung, collapsed lung, diabetes, rope burn on hand.

(Editor's Note: Under the "other" category, many of the particular items will have been recorded under a general category. For example, the climber who fell into his unanchored partner knocking him off would be coded as Fall on Rock, Falling Rock/Object, and Placed Inadequate Protection. The point in this category is to provide the reader with some added detail. It should be apparent that many of these details can be translated into a few basic categories.)

N.B. Also please note that the data for Month of Year for March was reported incorrectly for 1996. It should be the number 2, not 82.

MOUNTAIN RESCUE ASSOCIATION
OFFICERS

Tim Cochrane, *President*
PO Box 3480
Eagle, CO 81631

Tim Kovacs, *Vice-President*
PO Box 4004
Phoenix, AZ 85030

Tom Frazer, *Secretary/Treasurer*
4540 Saddlewood Dr.
Colorado Springs, CO 80918

Don Adamski, *Executive Officer*
6734 W. Multnomah Blvd.
Portland, OR 97223

Jon Inskeep, *Executive Officer*
Bubbling Well Lane
La Canada, CA 91011

MOUNTAIN RESCUE ASSOCIATION, INC.
710 10th St., Suite 105
Golden, CO 80401
970-328-5299

MOUNTAIN RESCUE GROUPS IN NORTH AMERICA

(Where not obvious, area covered is indicated in parentheses)
°Indicates membership in Mountain Rescue Association

ALASKA

Alaska Mountain Rescue Group,° PO Box 241102, Anchorage, AK 99524
U. S. Army Northern Warfare Training Center,° Fort Greeley, AK, APO Seattle 98733
Denali National Park Ranger Station, Talkeetna, AK 99676

ALBERTA

Banff Park Warden Service, Banff National Park, PO Box 900, Banff, Alberta T0L 0C0
Jasper Park Warden Service, Jasper National Park, PO Box 10, Jasper, Alberta T0E 1E0
Kananaskis Park Warden Service, Kananaskis Country, 201-800 Railway Ave.,
    Canmore, Alberta T1W1P1
Waterton Park Warden Service, Waterton National Park, Waterton, Alberta T0K 2M0

ARIZONA

Arizona Mountaineering Club Rescue Team, PO Box 1695, Phoenix, AZ 85030
Central Arizona Mountain Rescue Association,° PO Box 4004, Phoenix, AZ 85030
Grand Canyon National Park Rescue Team,° PO Box 129, Grand Canyon, AZ 86023
Southern Arizona Rescue Association, Inc.,° PO Box 12892, Tucson, AZ 85732
Sedona Fire Dept./Technical Rescue Group, PO Box 3964, West Sedona, AZ 86340

BRITISH COLUMBIA

Columbia Mountain Rescue Group, Royal Canadian Mounted Police, Invermere,
B.C. V0A 1K0 (East Kootenays)
Glacier Revelstoke Park Warden Service, Glacier Revelstoke National Park, PO Box
    350, Revelstoke, B.C. V0E 2S0)
Kootenay Park Warden Service, Kootenay National Park, PO Box 220, Radium Hot
    Springs, B.C. V0A 1M0
Mountain Rescue Group, c/o Frank Baumann, PO Box 1846, Squamish, B.C. V0N
    3G0 (Coast Range, Northern Cascades)
North Shore Rescue Team,° 165 East 13th Street, North Vancouver, B.C. V7L 2L3
YoHo National Park Warden Service, Box 99, Field, B.C., Canada V0A 1 GO

CALIFORNIA

Altadena Mountain Rescue Team, Inc.,° 780 E. Altadena Drive, Altadena, CA 91001
    (Los Angeles County)
Bay Area Mountain Rescue Unit, Inc.,° PO Box 6384, Stanford, CA 94309 (Northern
    Sierra Nevada)
China Lake Mountain Rescue Group,° PO Box 2037, Ridgecrest, CA 93555 (Southern
    Sierra Nevada)
De Anza Rescue Unit, PO Box 1599, El Centro, CA 92243 (Imperial Valley, Baja)
Inyo County Sheriff's Posse,° PO Box 982, Bishop, CA 93514
Joshua Tree National Monument SAR,° 74485 National Monument Dr., Twenty-nine
    Palms, CA 92277
Mono Lake County SAR, P. O. Box 436, June Lake, CA 93529

Los Padres Search and Rescue Team,° PO Box 30400, Santa Barbara, CA 93130
Malibu Mountain Rescue Team,° PO Box 222, Malibu, CA 90265
Montrose Search and Rescue Team,° PO Box 404, Montrose, CA 91021
(Los Angeles County)
Riverside Mountain Rescue Unit,° PO Box 5444, Riverside, CA 92517
(Riverside County)
Saddleback Search & Rescue Team, PO Box 5222, Orange, CA 92667
San Diego Mountain Rescue Team,° PO Box 81602, San Diego, CA 92138
San Dimas Mountain Rescue Team,° PO Box 35, San Dimas, CA 91733
San Gorgonio Search & Rescue Team, San Bernardino Sheriff, San Bernardino,
CA 92400 (San Bernardino Mountains)
Santa Clarita Valley Search and Rescue,° 23740 Magic Mountain Parkway, Valencia,
CA 91355
Sequoia-Kings Canyon National Park Rescue Team,° Three Rivers, CA 93271
Sierra Madre Search and Rescue Team,° PO Box 24, Sierra Madre, CA 91025
(Southwestern United States, Baja, California)
Yosemite National Park Rescue Team, Inc.° PO Box 577, Yosemite National Park,
CA 95389

COLORADO
Alpine Rescue Team, Inc.° PO Box 934, Evergreen, CO 80439 (Front Range)
Colorado Ground Search and Rescue,° 2391 S. Ash Street, Denver, CO 80222
Crested Butte Search and Rescue,° PO Box 485, Crested Butte, CO 81224
El Paso County Search & Rescue, Inc.,° PO Box 9922, Manitou Springs, CO 80932
Eldorado Canyon State Park,° PO Box B, Eldorado Springs, CO 80025
Garfield Search & Rescue,° PO Box 1116, Glenwood Springs, CO 81602
Grand County Search & Rescue,° PO Box 172, Winter Park, CO 80482
Larimer County Search & Rescue,° PO Box 1271, Fort Collins, CO 80522
Mountain Rescue—Aspen, Inc.° PO Box 4446, Aspen, CO 81612 (Western Slope)
Ouray Mountain Rescue Team, PO Box 220, Ouray, CO 81427 (Gunnison National
Park, Rio Grande National Forest, Uncompahgre Park)
Rocky Mountain National Park Rescue Team,° Estes Park, CO 80517
Rocky Mountain Rescue Group, Inc.,° PO Box Y, Boulder, CO 80306
San Juan Mountain SAR, PO Box 4, Silverton, CO 81433
Summit County Rescue Group,° PO Box 1794, Breckenridge, CO 80424
Vail Mountain Rescue Group,° PO Box 115, Vail, CO 81658
Western State Mountain Rescue Team,° Western State College, Gunnison, CO 81231

IDAHO
Idaho Mountain Search and Rescue,° PO Box 8714, Boise, ID 83707
Palouse-Clearwater Search and Rescue,° Route 1, Box 103-B, Troy, ID 83871

MAINE
Baxter State Park Mountain Rescue Team,° 64 Balsam Drive, Millinocket, ME 04462

MONTANA
Glacier National Park, SAR Coordinator, West Glacier, MT 59936
Lewis and Clark Search and Rescue,° PO Box 473, Helena, MT 59601

NEW HAMPSHIRE
Appalachian Mountain Club, Pinkham Notch Camp, Gorham, NH 03581 (White
    Mountains)
Mountain Rescue Service,° PO Box 494, North Conway, NH 03860

NEW MEXICO
Albuquerque Mountain Rescue Council,° PO Box 53396, Albuquerque, NM 87153
St. John's College Search and Rescue Team, 1160 Camino de Cruz Blanca, Santa Fe,
    NM 87501 (Northern New Mexico, Southern Colorado)

NORTHWEST TERRITORIES
Auyuittuq Park Warden Service, Auyuittuq National Park, Pangnirtung, N.W.T.
    X0A 0R0
Ellesmere Island Warden Service, Ellesmere Island National Park and Reserve,
P.O. Box 353, Pangnirtung, NT, XOA ORO

OREGON
Alpinees, Inc.,° 3571 Belmont Dr., Hood River, OR 97301 (Hood River County)
Corvallis Mountain Rescue Unit,° PO Box 116, Corvallis, OR 97339 (Central
    Cascades)
Crater Lake National Park Rescue Team, PO Box 7, Crater Lake, OR 97604
Eugene Mountain Rescue,° PO Box 10081, Eugene, OR 97401 (Oregon Cascades)
Hood River Crag Rates,° 1450 Nunamaker, Salem, OR 97031
Portland Mountain Rescue,° PO Box 1222, Portland, OR 97207

UTAH
American Search Dogs,° 4939 Benlomand, Ogden, UT 84003
Rocky Mountain Rescue Dogs,° 9624 S. 1210 E., Sandy, UT 84070
Salt Lake County Sheriff Search and Rescue,° 2942 Cardiff Road, Salt Lake
    City, UT 84121
Zion National Park°, Chief Ranger, Springdale, UT 84767

VERMONT
Mountain Cold Weather Rescue Team, Norwich University, Northfield, VT 05663
Stowe Rescue Squad, Stowe, VT 05672

VIRGINIA
Appalachian Search and Rescue Conference°, PO Box 430, Flint Hill, VA 22627
    (Blue Ridge and Shenandoah Mountains and Southwest Virginia)

WASHINGTON
Bellingham Mountain Rescue Council°, PO Box 292, Bellingham, WA 98225
    (Whatcom County)
Central Washington Mountain Rescue Council°, PO Box 2663, Yakima, WA 98907
    (Washington)
Everett Mountain Rescue Unit°, PO Box 2566, Everett, WA 98203 (North Central
    Cascades)

Mount Rainier National Park Rescue Team°, Longmire, WA 98397 (Mount Rainier National Park)

Seattle Mountain Rescue°, PO Box 67, Seattle, WA 98111 (Washington)

North Cascades National Park Rescue Team°, 2105 Highway 20, Sedro Woolley, WA 98284

Olympic Mountain Rescue°, PO Box 4244, Bremerton, WA 98312 (Olympic Range, Cascades)

Olympic National Park Rescue Team°, 600 Park Ave., Port Angeles, WA 98362 (Olympic National Park)

Skagit Mountain Rescue Unit°, 128 4th St., Mount Vernon, WA 98273 (Northern Cascades)

Tacoma Mountain Rescue Unit°, 7910 "A" St., Tacoma, WA 98408 (Central Washington, Cascades, Olympics)

WEST VIRGINIA
Gendarme/Seneca Rocks Climbing School, PO Box 23, Seneca Rocks, WV 26884
Pendelton County Tactical Skills Team, P.O. Box 727, WV 26807

WYOMING
Grand Teton National Park Mountain Search and Rescue Team°, PO Box 67, Moose, WY 83012 (Grand Teton National Park)
Mountain Rescue Outing Club, University of Wyoming, Laramie, WY 82071 (Wyoming)

YUKON
Kluane Park Warden Service, Kluane National Park, Haines Junction, Yukon Y0B 1L0